# *Das Haus*

Can Two Families — One Jewish,
One Gentile — Find Peace in a Clash
That Started in Nazi Germany?

By

J. Arthur Heise and Melanie Kuhr

*Das Haus*

MelArt
Copyright © 2013
All rights reserved
Dallas, TX/Hendersonville, NC
ISBN-13: 978-1481989268
ISBN-10: 148198926X

## Introduction

A novel this book is not. It just reads like one as it chronicles the odyssey of two families — both German, one Jewish, the other not — whose paths crossed in Nazi Germany and again nearly 70 years later in the United States in the quest for *das Haus* (the House).

It's a story that begins with the sale of a house by a German Jew to a German Gentile family in 1941. German law later presumed that all such sales by Jews were made under duress. In 1945, Soviet soldiers brutally confiscated the house to make it part of the Red Army's headquarters in what was to become East Germany. For nearly half a century, the house was the home of Russian military leaders and later the elite of the Stasi, the infamous East German security service, and other high-ranking officials of the *Deutsche Demokratische Republik (DDR)*.

Once the Berlin Wall came down, the heirs of each family sought to have the house returned to them. In the process, the German heir found

1

out that the German Jewish owners perished in the Theresienstadt concentration camp. In fact, the turbulent history of 20<sup>th</sup> century Germany, from just after World War I through the Nazi era, the Russian occupation of East Germany, the rise and fall of East Germany, all the way to the post-Cold War struggles to determine the rightful heirs to a property sold by a Jewish family to a member of the Nazi Party a half-century earlier, are all part of the story of *das Haus;* you will relive the terrible Battle for Berlin in which tens of thousands of Russian and German soldiers and civilians died and through which one of the heirs lived; you will accompany the heirs' families as they made their way to America under very trying circumstances; you will meet the "junkyard dog" lawyer without whom the quest for the house would have come to a screeching halt; and you will face the question of whether the father of the German heir was a strutting Nazi stalwart who stole the house. And you will find out how the two heirs, J. Arthur Heise and Melanie Kuhr, who started as antagonists in the 10-year battle over the ownership of the house, ended up friends and coauthors of this book.

You will also find that parts of the story were painful for each of the authors to write. But we decided to tell the story as it happened, not as we wish it had happened.

*Das Haus*

In memory of

**Theodor and Helene Simonsohn,
Holocaust victims**

# Contents

*Das Haus*

# 1: Out by Noon Tomorrow

**By J. Arthur Heise**

The banging on the front door got louder. BAM, BAM, BAM. Not knuckles on wood, but wood on wood. I had sneaked upstairs from the basement of our house, where my family had huddled for a couple of weeks to avoid the bullets, artillery shells, bombs and rockets that marked the Battle for Berlin.

We were caught in the middle of the final battle of World War II in the European theater, which lasted from mid-April into May 1945.

I was heading for the kitchen to find something to eat. Anything.

As I turned toward the front door, my Dad came racing up the stairs. "Stay away from that door," he yelled. The banging got louder. He slowly approached the door. I hid behind my father, scared but curious as only a six-year-old boy can be. When my father opened the door he was almost hit in the chest by the Russian's rifle butt.

There were two of them. One held the rifle with a bayonet mounted on it; the other clutched a submachine gun fitted with a big magazine drum. Both wore quilted jackets and trousers and fur caps — a round, red Soviet hammer and sickle emblem in the front — with the earflaps up.

They didn't want to come in — this time. The one with the rifle yelled in German, *"Raus, Morgen"* — Out, tomorrow — and then pointed to 12 on one of the half-dozen watches he was wearing on his left arm. They turned and left.

That curt order set in motion an odyssey of seven decades: An odyssey across the sea that cost thousands of dollars, awoke sometimes hurtful memories, renewed a childhood friendship and brought a new friend. Her name is Melanie Kuhr, the sole surviving heir to the house that I, Art Heise, was forced to abandon.

Now a corporate executive living in Texas, Melanie seemed to me initially indifferent to the history, legacy or circumstances surrounding the sale of the house. And as her involvement reluctantly deepened, her initial indifference shifted to skepticism and doubt, most notably of my motives. But as the saga continued to unfold, she was swept headlong into the quest, eventually becoming an enthused collaborator and now coauthor of this book. And so it was that the two of us, two skeptical strangers, would set forth to unravel the mysteries of *55 Neuwieder Strasse* in Berlin-Karlshorst, an odyssey in the quest for *das Haus.*

The house was in the middle-class Karlshorst suburb of Berlin. It was a two-family home with three rooms plus a small kitchen and bath on each floor — altogether about 2,200 square feet. We lived on the lower floor, and the upstairs was rented out to the Johns family.

We didn't know that the Red Army had decided to make Karlshorst its headquarters for what was to become East Berlin and the German Democratic Republic (*DDR*). Nor did we know that it was in Karlshorst — a couple of miles from our house — that Soviet Marshal

**Even after the Wall collapsed, signs marking the *Sperrgebiet* – restricted zone – were still in place but ignored.**

Georgy Zhukov on the night of May 8-9, 1945, signed the unconditional surrender of the Germans. The other Allies had signed the surrender documents the day before in Reims, France. Very quickly, most of the Karlshorst suburb was turned into a *Sperrgebiet* — restricted zone — encircled by high fences topped with barbed wire and guarded by armed patrols. Access to the area was *streng verboten* — strictly forbidden — until the Soviets moved out of some of the housing areas in the 1950s and 1960s.

My *Vati* — the affectionate term in German for Dad — and I went back to the basement. It was cramped because it had been divided into separate rooms. One was my father's small home workshop. We had moved everything against the walls and filled the center of the room with a small garden table and chairs. This is where *Vati*, my brother and I ate. In one corner was the heating system. A separate room was a coal cellar. The only light that streamed into the remaining open area — where we usually slept on the floor — came through one small window and two even smaller panes in a door that led to our backyard. We had hunkered down in the basement not only in fear of the artillery bombardment overhead, but also because of the Soviet soldiers who showed up at all hours, often drunk, looking for loot and women, age no matter.[1]

It was in that basement where I saw my father almost killed. It was mid-afternoon when a very drunk soldier showed up at the backyard door of the basement. He kept kicking the door with his boots while, on the other side, my father — small in stature, but very sinewy and muscular — put his shoulder where he anticipated the next kick to land.

The Russian finally quit his kicking. Instead, he smashed one of the two small windows at the top of the door with his bayonet. He stood there with the bayonet poking through the broken window. With glazed eyes, he stared at my father who, to my amazement, stared back. The bayonet was two to three inches from my father's face. The soldier yelled in Russian, his

---

[1] For detailed information on the behavior of the Red Army in Germany, see Norman M. Naimark, *The Russians in Germany* (Cambridge, Mass.: Belknap Press of Harvard University, 1995), and Anonymous, *A Woman in Berlin* (New York: Metropolitan Books, 2005).

words slurred. Although the staring contest lasted only a moment, it seemed forever to me. I shook with fear. Then the soldier turned and left. My father found some boards and nailed the basement door shut.

The coal cellar was about 10 feet by 10 feet, as I recall. Most of the scarce coal was gone because it was May, and what little remained had been swept into a corner and covered with cardboard. Old blankets covered the floor of the coal cellar, and pillows were strewn about.

For two weeks, it had become home for a half-dozen women and small children from the neighborhood. At the time, I didn't fully understand why the women — all dressed in rumpled clothes and dark scarves — were there, except that the Russians were doing something to women that they were very afraid of. I do remember one day a woman's voice crying outside our house, *"Frau Heise, Hilfe, Hilfe"* (Mrs. Heise, help, help). My mother had a reputation in the neighborhood for being steady and resolute when an emergency arose; for instance, when one of the neighbor's boys fell off his bicycle and broke his arm, my mother rushed to his aid and accompanied the boy's mother to the hospital. I never forgot that cry for *Hilfe, Hilfe* that my mother didn't answer. Years later, I asked her why she had not responded to the cry. The Russians had caught the woman and were going to rape her, she explained to me. If my mother had tried to help, she would have suffered the same fate.

During the day, the women would come out of the coal cellar only briefly to use the bathroom and to wash soiled diapers. During the dark of night, they would sneak through the backyards to prepare food at their own homes as best they could for their older children and older male relatives who lived with them. Most husbands and older sons were in the military. My mother would do the same. She would go to the kitchen after dark and without turning on a light — just the gas stove — fix whatever little we were going to eat that evening and the next day. Usually my father, brother and I would sit together for our meager meals on garden chairs in my father's former workshop while my mother was back in the coal cellar.

**Dozens of Soviet T-34 tanks like this one lined Art's street in Berlin-Karlshorst. The tank above is on display at the Russian-German museum in Berlin-Karlshorst.**

We lived on watery vegetable or potato soup and a slice or two of dark bread, the only food available — and intermittently, at that — via ration cards.

I often stood on a box to look through the small window of the coal cellar at the row of Soviet tanks that stretched the length of our street. What scared me more than the tanks were the soldiers lolling around the tanks. I had never seen people like that. They had pitch-black hair, slanted eyes to match, and skin darker than mine. In their quilted jackets and pants, they looked to my 6-year-old eyes as if they were from another world. When I climbed down from my box, my hands were black from the coal dust that still covered the windowsill.

The door to the coal cellar was hidden behind an old European-style wardrobe that my father now strained to shove aside. He opened the door to let my mother, the neighborhood women and the small children out. My brother, Norbert, was not among them, but my father knew where he was. "Go up to the *Dachstube*

**The small window on the left is the window to the coal cellar from which Art watched the Soviet tanks lining his street and the troops lolling around them.**

(attic room) and get your brother." Despite my father's orders, my 10-year-old brother Norbert would sneak up to the dormer window in the attic to get a better view of the Soviets up and down our street.

By the time I returned with Norbert, my father had already told everyone about the soldier's order: "All of us have to be out of the house by noon tomorrow."

The adults all talked at once. Where do we go? What can we take? There are no cars, buses or trains. How do we go?

As usual, my *Mutti* — the affectionate term in German for Mom — eventually calmed everyone down. Go home through the backyards, where all the fences had openings cut into them so no one had to walk on the street to get from house to house, she said. Pack what you can carry. If you have any heavy valuables you want to store in what might be a safe place, bring them over and we'll put them in the *Sickergrube.* (The *Sickergrube* was a former septic tank that my father had thoroughly cleaned and lined with brick to store wine.) When it's full, we'll cover the lid with manure, my mother said. She had the load of manure delivered a few weeks earlier for her roses but mainly for her *Gemüsegarten* — the vegetable garden where she grew everything from kohlrabi to tomatoes, everything that ration cards wouldn't buy. When my mother assured the women that the manure would hide the entrance to the *Sickergrube,* she assumed we would be back in the house in a few weeks, at most a few months.

After everyone had left, we searched for suitcases, heavy cloth bags, including some long forgotten potato sacks. Two Persian carpets, the family silver and the good china went into the *Sickergrube*. I don't recall where or how, but my father came up with a pushcart on which we would load most of the belongings we could take.

The house did hold some good memories for me. We moved into it in 1941 as the war began to intensify. I remember events starting sometime in 1943 or 1944, when I was five years old, fortunately too young to be forced into the Hitler Youth. Some of the memories involved activities typical of children that age. Friends and I would play hopscotch or soccer on the quiet street or have snowball fights and build snowmen in the winter. Or, if the weather was bad, we would play indoors. A favorite was my brother's toy train. But we could play with it only when he was in school. He had it set up exactly the way he wanted it, and we would invariably mess it up in some way, earning his wrath.

Most of my memories of the house, however, were unpleasant.

There was the time, for instance, when the official air raid alarms were already unreliable and we were caught in the open on the way to the government bomb shelter. The shortcut we used was not a road, just a path over some sandy soil. A bomb hit somewhere near us — I have no idea how near — but close enough to toss all of us 10 or 20 feet through the air. Thanks to landing on the sandy ground, we suffered only a few cuts and bruises.

Many a night when we came out of the bunker at three or four o'clock in the morning, the sky was as bright as if it were noon. But the sky was not blue. It was orangey-red as far as I could see, and we had trouble standing up against the howling wind as the fires sucked the oxygen from the air. All of Berlin, it seemed, was on fire. Since it was night, the devastation was most likely caused by British planes that carpet-bombed entire districts of the city. During the day, the bombers were typically American; they precision-bombed specific targets, factories or government buildings. Oh, how I feared those bombers, whether the British by night or the Americans by day.

As a consequence, I suffered serious sleep problems that haunted me until I was 12 or 13. I would toss from side to side for a half-hour or so to rock myself to sleep. And from time to time, I wet myself when the air raid alarm woke me from a deep sleep.

As the war went on, the air raid alerts became less and less reliable. So my father and some neighbors decided to build their own air raid shelter in our backyard. My *Vati* was a master electrician with his own small business repairing and building electrical motors and switching gear. He had not been drafted into the *Wehrmacht* (army) because his small factory was considered essential to the war effort. He was also very good at mathematics and very good with his hands.

When the plan was hatched for the backyard air raid shelter, my father carefully considered its design. As the air raids intensified and the warning sirens became all but useless, the government started to furnish building material for people to build their own shelters. The material consisted basically of lengths of dove-tailed, steel-reinforced concrete that were perhaps four or five inches thick and about a foot-and-a-half tall. They could be assembled quickly by a few men and women in a hole they had dug in the ground.

But as he moved about Berlin in the course of his work, my father noticed that when a bomb came down near one of these shelters, the concrete would often break and crush everyone inside.

So he turned to a former customer who was in the business of building large wooden fishing boats. Bartering with him, my father secured two types of oak lumber — some planks that were about six inches by 12 inches and some eight-by-eight beams.

He and the neighbors dug the hole and placed the beams so that they would form a rectangle at three-foot or so intervals. The planks went behind and atop the beams, exits with ladders were placed at both ends, and a large tub of water — in case of fire in the shelter — was installed. All the dirt from the hole was placed on top of the shelter. Benches on either side were narrow and so close that you had to dovetail your legs with the person across from you.

On the street behind our house was a block-long, three-story apartment building, less than 200 feet from the shelter. One night when we were in the shelter, a bomb hit the apartment building.

When the first shock wave from the bomb rocked the shelter, I was sure we would all die. The oak planks and beams croaked and screeched and closed in on us. But then, slowly, ever so slowly, they flexed back. The next shock wave bent them inward again, but not as far. Not a word was said, not a scream uttered, as we listened to the groaning oak. It held.

When we emerged from the shelter in the morning, we were terrified to find an incendiary bomb, six feet or so long, sticking out of the dirt atop the shelter. It had been a dud.

To this day, there are times when I can hear the creaking planks and feel them coming toward me.

So I did not cry when we were finished packing — mostly food and clothing — and ready to head to my grandmother's house, which was on the other side of the sprawling city.

As we departed, *Mutti* frantically scoured the house one last time to make sure we didn't forget something essential. The last thing she

**This is the picture of das Haus, with the front dormer window half-open, which Art's mother grabbed as they evacuated the house and of which Melanie – mysteriously – has an identical copy.**

stuffed in a suitcase on that morning of May 10, 1945, was a framed picture of our house, a house I would not see again for nearly 50 years. And it took me an additional 10 years to get the house back. Ten years of research, wrangling with lawyers and bureaucrats — and encountering two chilling surprises.

*Das Haus*

## 2: Utterly Despicable Behavior

**By J. Arthur Heise**

As we set out for my grandmother's house, the narrow wheels of the heavily loaded pushcart left tracks in the soft asphalt. It was one of the hottest days in Berlin's history. As we came closer to the center of the city, more and more streets were covered in rubble from the bombing and artillery fire. Some were closed, forcing us to make circuitous detours. When my short legs gave out, I rode on the cart that my *Vati* and Norbert pushed along with streams of hundreds of other refugees moving in every direction.

The smell of the city ranged from unpleasant to unbearable. It was a combination of the odor given off by decomposing bodies crushed beneath the rubble, smoke from smoldering buildings and the stench from broken sewer lines. We finally stopped late in the day at the apartment of some friends, where we spent the night in the cellar of the building.

Berlin had been under merciless attack by artillery, Katyushka rockets (nicknamed "Stalin Organs" because of the screaming noise they made while airborne), small-arms fire and aerial attacks for days.

**A truck-mounted launcher of the feared Soviet Katyushka rockets. It could fire 16 rockets at a time. It is now on display in the Russian-German museum in Karlshorst.**

When the Soviet troops pushed into the city, it was largely populated by women. Of an estimated civilian population of 2.7 million at war's end, more than 2 million were women. The central part of the city had been leveled either by the incessant attacks by the British and American air forces in the years before the Soviet onslaught and now by the "merciless shelling that had no pattern." Knowing the war was lost, the Nazis had blown up 120 of the city's 248 bridges to slow down the advancing Russians, but also, as part of Hitler's scorched earth policy, to make life even more miserable for the remaining Berliners.[2]

Soldiers of the Red Army were merciless in their treatment of the German population. Given the gruesome behavior of the Germans when they invaded Eastern Europe and the Soviet Union and their scorched earth policy when they were forced to retreat, that cruel behavior is perhaps understandable.

The suffering of the Soviets is made clear by the casualties they suffered during World War II. Even today the estimates of military and civilian deaths vary widely for the Soviet Union and Nazi Germany. The Soviets lost an

---

[2] I have drawn in this section and elsewhere on what I believe is the best account of the Battle for Berlin: Cornelius Ryan, *The Last Battle* (New York: Simon and Schuster, 1966).

estimated 10 to 13 million civilians; an estimated two million German civilians were killed. Depending on the source, between six million and 10 million Soviet soldiers were killed, as were about 3.5 million German soldiers.[3] In the Battle for Berlin alone, the Soviets suffered approximately 300,000 casualties, including 70,000 to 80,000 dead,[4] while German losses in the battle are estimated at 150,000 to 170,000

While the fury Soviet soldiers vented upon Berlin's civilians is perhaps understandable, it was also utterly despicable.

"The taking of Berlin was accompanied by an unrestrained explosion of sexual violence by Soviet soldiers."[5] Just how many women were violated remains unclear, although some claim that a majority of Berlin women were attacked.

---

[3] These figures are all estimates. See Second World War History.com: *World War II Casualty Statistics*; War Chronicle.com, *Estimated war dead World War II*; Infoplease.com , *Casualties in World War II*; and Olive-Drab.com, *1945: Berlin*.
[4] See also Frederick Taylor, *Exorcising Hitler* (New York: Bloomsbury Press, 2011), xxvii.
[5] Naimark, *The Russians in Germany,* 79-80.

An excerpt from the diary of a Swiss journalist illustrates the brutality of the attacks:

> In one case a father tries to protect a child, a young girl. The Mongols [the generic term for Soviet Central Asians] stick a three-edged bayonet in his gut. The Russians stand in lines of dozens in front of lone women. In their eagerness, they don't even notice that they [the women] are dying, perhaps because they have swallowed poison or from internal bleeding of the organs. Many women bite and scratch to defend themselves, but they are hit over the head with gun butts. Men throw themselves at the soldiers but are dispatched in no time with a shot. Women and girls are chased in gardens and through the streets, followed on top of roofs and the pursued jump [for their lives]....[6]

---

[6] See Naimark, *The Russians in Germany*, p. 82.

That was the state of Berlin as we struggled to reach my grandmother's house. My mother wore a large, dark headscarf that hid not only her hair but also most of her face. And she wore the frumpy, dirt-flecked clothes that she used when gardening. Anything to appear unattractive. That strategy, along with a lot of luck, worked: She was not raped.

A surprise awaited us when we arrived at my grandmother's late the next day: It and several of her neighbors' homes also had been taken over by the Soviets. We joined six other families who were jammed in one of the unoccupied houses. Fortunately, the soldiers left after a week. Unfortunately, they left a stinking mess behind. When the toilet in my grandmother's house plugged up, the Russians used the bathtub instead, leaving it half full of excrement. It was obvious that many of the soldiers had no idea of how to use modern facilities. Indeed, legend had it that there were incidents when the Soviet soldiers would rip a faucet out of the wall to take it home, stick it in the wall and expect running water to come out.

One day, some weeks later, when we were still at my grandmother's house, I had a moment that initially left me trembling with fear. My mother — still in her frumpy get-up — and I were walking to a neighbor's house when we ran into a Russian soldier, well over six feet tall, broad-shouldered and blond. He started talking to my mother in broken German. He wanted to do something with me. He picked me up, tossed me playfully in the air, hugged me and kissed me on both cheeks. He told my mother he had a boy my age of his own back in the Soviet Union and missed him terribly.

During all this time, my father was scouring Berlin to find us a permanent place to stay — a tough challenge in a city that lay in ruins. But eventually he found out that a small apartment right where his business had been for years might become available. He knew the owner of the building well, and things were worked out.

While we were lucky to have a place of our own, we didn't realize until weeks later just how lucky we were. While we knew that the Allies had agreed to break up Germany into four zones, no one knew yet how Berlin was going to be divided.

When the dividing lines for the city were announced, by pure chance our apartment turned out to be one block inside the American sector. That turned out to be a life-changing event for me.

Even during the war, my father had talked about his brother, Walter, who lived in the United States. Uncle Walter had left Germany in the Twenties, lived in Cuba for a time and then moved to America. They had not seen each other since my uncle had left Germany. My father was sick of living in Germany: When he was a boy, he lived through World War I; then came the political turmoil of the Twenties; then the Great Depression, when it took a wheelbarrow full of *Reichsmarks*, as legend has it, to buy a loaf of bread; then came

Hitler, World War II and the Holocaust in which six million Jews and five million Roma (gypsies), political prisoners, homosexuals, Russians, Germans, Poles and others were slaughtered. Again and again, he would say that he did not want his sons to experience what he had. He wanted out; he wanted to go to America.

Once things had settled down a bit after the war and the post office was operating again, my father decided to try to contact Uncle Walter. Courtesy of what was then the U.S. Post Office, my father found his brother in America. The only address my father had for his brother was an old, pre-war address in New York City. But the post office forwarded the letter correctly to his brother's new address in Syracuse, New York.

My father asked his brother to sponsor us so we could emigrate to America. Uncle Walter responded not only with packages filled with chocolate, candy bars, canned meats and cigarettes, but he was also willing, nay, eager to sponsor us to come to America.

When the first package arrived, *Mutti* spread the goodies on my parents' bed and all four of us stared in wonder. The cigarettes served two purposes. The first was to sate *Vati's* own habit; the second was for bartering on the black market. Few items had more value on Berlin's black market than American cigarettes. My mother would cut the candy bars in half and my brother Norbert and I each got a half on the spot and the rest after dinner the next few evenings.

But a big problem stood in the way of our obtaining a U.S. family visa.

Like most owners of businesses, small or large, my father had been forced to join the Nazi Party. For example, even the heroic Oscar Schindler was not only a member of the Nazi Party, but he also agreed to be a spy for German counterintelligence, "because as an *Abwehr* agent, he was exempt from army service." Indeed, at one point he boasted that "I'm an essential war producer" and therefore exempt from military service. [7] It is highly improbable that Schindler would have been able to save the hundreds of Jews working in his war-essential factory had he not been in the party nor served as a spy.

But having been a party member meant that my father had to be "denazified," a procedure established by the Allies and strongly enforced in the American sector by the Office of Military Government, Berlin Sector, Public Safety—Special Branch. Without a finding that he was not a Nazi Party *Bonze* (big wig), a visa to emigrate to the United States was not in the cards.

It was not until fall of 1947 that my father was "denazified" when the American Office of Military Government found that he was "only a nominal Nazi." It was not until 57 years later that I learned exactly what that meant — when I did some serious soul-searching about what it meant to have a father who was a Nazi, even if only a "nominal" one.

---

[7] Thomas Keneally, *Schindler's List* (New York: Simon & Schuster, 1982) 39, 114.

Having been "denazified" didn't mean a U.S. visa was forthcoming any time soon. There was paperwork to be filled out, interviews to attend, medical exams of the entire family to be completed and a long waiting list for each of these steps. At the medical exam — my father who could stare down a Russian bayonet — fainted when he was poked with a needle to extract some blood. (To this day, I can't watch when I receive a blood test or injection.) And there were visa quotas. We had to wait our turn.

Meanwhile, life in the devastated city began to stir. Mostly women, the *Trümmerfrauen* (rubble women) began to collect the rubble by hand to open the many blocked streets. Food was scarce. There were ration cards, but they did not go very far. Potatoes were the staple. Through his business connections, my father bartered for several sacks of soybean meal that my mother tried in every conceivable way to turn into something that was appetizing. She made soybean soup, soybean bread, soybean cake, soybean pancakes and anything else she could think of. But in the end it all tasted like soybean meal — in short, like *Scheisse.*

In 1946, I enjoyed the best meal I would have in my entire life — better than any dish I have eaten in the five-dozen years since in some of the best restaurants in the United States, Europe, the Middle East and Latin America.

There was a rumor in our neighborhood that some Canadian wheat and American butter had arrived in Berlin. My brother was dispatched to the neighborhood bakery two streets away; I was sent to the little grocery store around the corner. We joined the long lines that had already formed.

We both arrived at home at nearly the same moment, he with an arm full with freshly baked, large loaves of crisp white bread, I with two pounds of fresh American butter. We couldn't wait for *Mutti* to cut the bread. As the youngest, I was awarded the first heel she cut. I slathered it with butter, a quarter of an inch thick. When I bit into it, the crust crackled in my mouth as the butter melted. One heel was not enough; I had another slice and then another. With one of the large loaves completely gone, the four of us sat there, full of something delicious for the first time in a long time. It was a heavenly meal.

Besides the scarce food situation, there was the problem of staying warm in the winter. The winter of 1947 was one of the coldest on record in Germany. Our apartment, like most of that era, had a *Kachelofen*, a floor-to-ceiling oven-like contraption clad in tile that was fed with wood or coal. But there was no coal or wood. Fortunately, my father's factory contained a lot of wooden crates for screws, nuts and machinery parts. All the boards from the crates went up the chimney that winter. Electricity was another problem. It would come on for a few irregular hours on some days and not at all on others. Using his ingenuity once again, *Vati* bartered for an old diesel generator, which he set up in his factory, behind the apartment house where we lived. It had a flywheel so heavy that the men did not trust the elevator to carry it up to the third floor. Instead, they used a heavy rope and pulley to hoist it three flights and brought it in through a disassembled window.

**Art's father at work in his small electrical motor and equipment factory.**

So now my father had electricity during the day to run his factory. He also figured out a way to wire the generator into the electrical system of the apartment house. Thus, every evening everyone in the building had electricity for a couple of hours. Where did he get the diesel fuel? Bartering on the black market, of course.

My parents also wanted my brother and me to have as normal a life as was possible under the circumstances. One thing they wanted us to do was to learn to play musical instruments. My brother was assigned the piano, and I the violin. Both of us took lessons, but Norbert had a natural talent for the piano. In the evening, when the U.S. Armed Forces Network regularly aired a jazz program, my brother was glued to the radio. If he heard a piece he liked, he would sit down at the piano and play the tune by ear.

I wasn't quite as good with the violin. In fact, after several weeks of private instruction, my violin teacher showed up at our apartment one evening. He wanted to see my father. *Vati* invited him in, and my music teacher hemmed and hawed a bit before he worked up the courage to explain his visit.

*"Herr* Heise," he told my father, "as you know times are bad and my income is very limited. But your son's attempt to play the violin is

hopeless. As much as I need the money, I don't need it that badly."

Thus ended my musical career.

Otherwise, life began to take on some form of normality for my brother and me. We would race our bicycles, cycle across town in the summer to go swimming in the pool of Berlin's Olympic Stadium and, led by my brother, four or five of us boys would explore bombed-out ruins of apartment buildings, stores and factories.

In one derelict warehouse of the Berlin subway, we found a box full of odd-shaped keys. My brother, always a bit of a rascal, figured out that these keys opened the driver's cabin of the subway trains that were beginning to run again. Naturally, Norbert had to try one of the keys and got into the driver's cabin — only to be nabbed by the police. An officer promptly showed up at our apartment to have a serious conversation with my brother and my parents. In the end, all the officer wanted was for Norbert to take him to where we had found the keys. He did so, and the authorities forgot the episode.

Life became tough again in 1948, when the Soviets decided to blockade Berlin by prohibiting all train and truck travel in and out of the city. The Soviets' aim was to take over Berlin, which was surrounded by what by now had become East Germany or, more formally, the German Democratic Republic, a puppet state controlled by the U.S.S.R.

Food and fuel became scarce again. But the Western Allies, especially the United States, wouldn't buckle. Instead President Harry S Truman started the Berlin Airlift to feed and warm residents of the western part of Berlin. Between June 1948 and May 1949, about 200,000 flights flew food and fuel into the beleaguered city, many days bringing in as much as 4,700 tons of cargo.[8]

---

[8] Gary B. Nash, *The American People: Creating a Nation and a Society* (New York: Pearson Longman, 2008) 828.

Most of the planes heading for Tempelhof Airport flew directly over our apartment house at low altitude, one every few minutes, day and night. We loved the racket they made.

Although the airport was a few miles away, some of my friends and I regularly headed for the fence that ran atop a berm encircling part of Tempelhof. Lots of other kids our age were there hoping to catch one of the handmade parachutes attached to candy bars that some of the pilots threw out of the cockpit as they approached the runway. When one of the little parachutes came down, there was a mad scramble. Some of the lucky ones who caught a parachute shared the three or four candy bars that were attached. Others grabbed their loot and took off as fast as they could. I never caught one.

**Art bicycling around his neighborhood in Berlin about a year after the airlift.**

Eventually the American flight crews dropped hundreds of the little parachutes all over West Berlin. Thousands of pounds of candy and handkerchiefs were contributed by individual Americans and U.S. candy manufacturers. The little parachutes were a visible symbol of the airlift and the support of West Berlin by the Allies, especially the Americans, and helped turn the attitude of West Berliners from one of fear and loathing into one of appreciation and gratitude.[9] And that included me.

In 1952, I started my first year in high school and my last year in Germany.

We had finally been granted a visa to go to the United States of America.

---

[9] See Andrei Cherny, *The Candy Bombers* (New York: G.P. Putnam, 2008).

*Das Haus*

## 3: Coming to America

**By J. Arthur Heise**

We arrived in Canada in October 1953. We sailed to Quebec City because it was the earliest passage my father could secure after receiving the visa earlier that year. But the North Atlantic in October was not kind to me. I was seasick for eight of the 10 days it took to reach Canada. All I could keep down while lying on my bunk were slices of white bread and small orange wedges.

In Quebec, my father's brother and wife greeted us in a huge pre-war car with a roomy trailer attached. They brought the trailer because we had several crates of belongings, including two sets of expensive German china, Rosenthal and Hutchenreuther. My father brought the china and two costly cameras because there were limits on the amount of cash that could be taken out of post-war Germany. He intended to turn the cameras and the china into cash for us to live on during our first months in America.

My aunt and uncle seemed much older than I had expected, especially my uncle, who looked pale and clearly ill to me.

When we arrived in Syracuse, New York, the nightmare started. Initially, we were to stay at my uncle's small, two-story house. They had not bothered to look for a place where we could live. The reason became clear once we walked into the house. They had started to renovate it, and many of the walls had been stripped to the studs. It was soon obvious that, because of my uncle's poor health, we were expected to rebuild the place in exchange for staying.

That was just the beginning of the ordeal. My uncle had written to my father that he also had a small electrical motor and equipment business that he wanted my father to run because he was too ill to continue to do so himself.

*Vati's* face was ashen when he returned from a visit to the small factory. He took the family for a walk and explained to us what he had found. The factory had not been operating for some time, and all the equipment was covered in dust. There seemed to be no customers. So what did my aunt and uncle live on? They must have had substantial resources because the affidavit they had to execute for us to come to the United States required proof of their financial ability in case they had to support us. I never heard an answer to that question.

In short, there was no factory for my father to run and support his family. We were on our own to start a new life.

Given what had greeted us, the atmosphere in the house became tense. My aunt, Ellen, was particularly nasty to my brother and me, bossing us around every chance she had. My uncle was no better, finding fault with whatever we tried to do to help fix up the house. Norbert and I referred to our aunt as *"die Hexe"* (the witch) and my uncle as *"das Arschloch"* (the asshole). The relationship between my aunt and uncle and my parents was no better. Indeed, at one point my mother became so upset that she stormed out of the house, screaming that she was going to throw herself under a bus. She didn't, and we found my *Mutti* a few blocks away on a bus stop bench, tears streaming from her reddened eyes.

The neighbors were aware of the condition of my uncle's house and his wife's general unfriendliness. Some came to meet us, and others greeted us on the street.

Our priority was to find our own place to live. One of the neighbors, the elderly Mr. Taylor, was in the real estate business and helped us find a small apartment. Another, Mr. Bean, an engineer at a General Electric plant then in Syracuse, gave my father tips on where to look for a job in which he could bring his extensive skills to bear.

The second priority was to find jobs for everyone. Money was running out, and selling the china and cameras turned out to be more difficult than anticipated. The cameras — a Leica and a Contax — sold quickly but at bargain-basement prices. The Rosenthal china took a bit longer and went for a low price. Nobody seemed to have heard of Hutchenreuther china. As a result, it serves as my family's "good" china to this day.

The big problem in my father's job hunt was his limited English. So my brother — who had graduated from high school just before we left Germany — and I — who had one year of high school English — took turns accompanying him as translators when he went to a job interview. It was humiliating for him, going from a successful small business owner to a job seeker who had to rely on his sons to translate. Eventually, he found a job with a Westinghouse facility in Syracuse that built highly specialized electrical motors. He slowly learned English by going to night school.

*Mutti*, who had been a *Hausfrau* all of her life, found a job at a dry cleaner owned by a German-American family. It was brutally hot work, especially in the summer, but she knew we needed the money.

Norbert found employment as a machinist at a factory owned by another German-American. Even I found a job, washing windows and doing yard work for the next-door neighbors, the Beans, and other folks living on the street. Eventually, while going to high school and later attending college part-time, I worked — because my father had determined that I should become an engineer — in the chemistry lab of Crouse Hinds, the company that made virtually every traffic light in the United States at the time, and then in the experimental lab at Porter-Cable, a power tool manufacturer.

My English needed major improvement before I could resume high school. A group of mostly gray-haired women — retired teachers, librarians, well-educated homemakers — called themselves the Americanization League, and they had as their mission teaching English to immigrants like me. So off I went, five mornings a week, to the Syracuse YWCA to learn English one-on-one with some of the nicest, most patient women I have ever met.

After three months, the high school decided I was ready to resume my studies. My biggest problem was that the State of New York required four years of high school English. I squeezed that into a little under two years because I wanted to graduate and find a full-time job.

After my year in a German high school, I found the American high school a cinch. I had never heard of study halls in Germany. You went from class to class, took your books home and did two or three hours of homework.

Here, I never took a book home. My father, who by this time had bought a used car, would drop me off at the high school on his way to work, giving me an hour to do homework before my first class. And I had all those hours in study halls.

My other problem was the anti-German sentiment I sometimes encountered. I could understand that, because some of my classmates had a father, brother or uncle killed or injured during World War II. But when one of the school's bullies called me a "dirty German" in front of a group of my friends, I lost it. A right hook, which I didn't know I had, floored him.

Off I went to the office of the school's disciplinarian, the vice principal. He listened to my story and that of the bully. I was awarded three days of after-school detention. A few days after serving the detention, I was called back to the vice principal's office. He told me he understood why I decked the other kid, but since I threw the first punch he had no choice but to punish me.

More important, though, he had reviewed my academic record and asked me about my family's travails after arriving in the U.S. He decided that there had to be a college scholarship out there somewhere for me. He looked hard and long on my behalf but always came up against a wall: The applicant had to be a U.S. citizen, which I could not yet become. The vice principal seemed almost as disappointed as I was. Although it didn't help with the scholarships, I became a U.S. citizen at the earliest opportunity, on December 9, 1959.

I still spoke English with an accent after high school. While working in the experimental lab at Porter Cable, I developed a plan to deal with that. My fellow workers, all highly accomplished craftsmen, kept making fun of my pronunciation problems. One day, as eight or ten of us sat around the communal lunch table, I asked that instead of making fun of the way I spoke, they should correct me on the spot and teach me the correct pronunciation.

They took their new teaching role seriously. They corrected me a dozen times a day. My long-term aim was to speak English like a native. In the years to come, when I was in the South, people thought I was from the North; when I was on the East Coast, people thought I was from the Midwest. Rarely does anyone today detect the slight German accent that sometimes sneaks into my speech.

Although my high school yearbook has me saying that I wanted to be an electrical engineer, I was not at all enthralled by my father's idea. For one thing, when I took the required chemistry and physics courses while attending Syracuse University part-time, I really struggled. In the physics course, I ended up with a D minus minus. I had never seen a D minus minus, so I sought out the professor for an explanation. It was simple, he said. Since it was a university-required course, had he given me an F, he would have to put up with me again in his class next year. But with a D minus minus, I had fulfilled the requirement — he was happy and so was I.

When I finally saved enough money and got some help from my parents to attend Syracuse full-time, I switched my major to what really interested me: journalism and political science. I didn't tell my father for a year. When I finally did, I put my grade reports from the past year in front him so he could compare them with the grades I had earned earlier. He was convinced when he saw that As and a few Bs had replaced Cs, Ds and that D minus minus. Indeed, I stayed at Syracuse University to earn a master's degree in mass communication.

The main reason I stayed for the master's degree was not just a thirst for knowledge. On April 13, 1960, I had met the most charming and exotic woman — who at the time had a ponytail that reached her waist — who also attended Syracuse.

**Art's wife of 50 years, shortly after he met her at Syracuse University.**

She was Persian and could dance like an angel. And she had an exotic name: Simine. But she was a year behind me and so I asked the Air Force — I had been commissioned a second lieutenant after completing Air Force ROTC — for a one-year deferment to earn my master's degree. But what I really wanted was to stay with the woman I knew would one day become my wife.

While pursuing my undergraduate degree, I had joined the Air Force Reserve Officer Training Corps. Besides wanting to be a journalist, I also dreamed of flying fighter jets. The first time I came home to my parents' house — where I lived while pursuing my undergraduate work — in my uniform, my usually calm, soft-spoken father went ballistic.

"What are you doing in that uniform? All my life," he fumed, "I have hated uniforms because they bring nothing but war and devastation." I tried to persuade him that in America, things were different, and that it was honorable to serve one's country. He nodded, but was never convinced.

My father did not serve in the military during World War II because, as I already noted, his factory was considered essential to the war effort. Despite that exemption from military service, the Brownshirts of the Nazi Party kept trying to haul him off to the *Wehrmacht* (German army). It became so ridiculous, as my father would recall with a chuckle, that at one point the *Luftwaffe* (air force), for which he had to do some work, posted an armed sentry at the door of his factory to keep him from being "recruited" into the *Wehrmacht.*

After working hard for several years, my mother adjusted to a better life in America. She became a *Hausfrau* again when my parents were financially able to reach for the American dream. In 1958, they bought a small three-bedroom, one-bath rancher in the suburbs of Syracuse. She was happy keeping the house spotless, planting two flower gardens — the one in the back of the house all roses, of course, just as in Karlshorst — cooking, baking and putting on table-bending feasts for Easter and Christmas.

**Art's parents, Annemarie and Arthur, in their first house in America.**

The story of my brother turned out less sunny. Norbert wanted to get rich fast. After completing his full-time day job at a Chrysler factory in Syracuse, he would race 45 miles to another plant in Rome, N.Y., and work the nightshift as a machinist.

One reason for his hectic schedule was that he wanted to bring his high school sweetheart from Germany to marry her. But the other

**Art's brother Norbert relaxing in his *Lederhosen***

reasons were that he liked cars and women. Norbert was constantly bragging that he was going to get two Ph.Ds., one in physics and the ther in electrical engineering so one day he could run his own large company. Instead, he flunked out of college before completing his first year.

He married his sweetheart from Germany in the mid-1950s and they moved to Spotswood, New Jersey, so that he could be near a job he had taken with an insurance company in New York City. His marriage began to falter rapidly. When I saw him at Christmas 1964, he was deeply depressed. He lay on the couch all day, pretending to sleep. Simine, my wife, tried to cheer him up and keep him busy playing cards. Nothing worked. I thought the state of his marriage was the cause. I counseled him to end the marriage since neither he nor his wife was happy. I made no impression. Also, my father – in the old-school German tradition —

Art as executive officer of the library at the U.S. Air Force Academy.

was vehemently opposed to divorce.

While working for the insurance company,

Norbert constantly tried to get involved in other businesses, mostly involving Germany and, I learned later, a $100-million construction project in Montreal. It fell through. So did a big job with a firm in Germany for which he had applied. He traveled back and forth to Germany, Canada and various U.S. cities, spending large amounts of money, large enough that he had to borrow from my father to keep his creditors at bay. And although he knew that his parents were struggling to prepare for their retirement, he never paid them back. What his German business ventures entailed remains unclear to this day. Ultimately, my brother's situation went beyond desperate. On May 15, 1965, at the age of 31, he ran a vacuum cleaner hose from the exhaust pipe of his Volkswagen into the car and committed suicide. There was no suicide note, only a request that his remains be cremated.

I was in Spotswood the next day, courtesy of the U.S. Air Force. My sister-in-law asked me to go through his papers so she would have some idea where she stood financially. While going through his files, I found no clues about his extracurricular activities other than a few letters to companies — all in Germany — inquiring about some product or other. But I did find evidence of a mountain of debt, mostly to credit card companies, including two suits filed against him by creditors. I also found a life insurance policy that could cover much of that debt.

Much to my surprise, not long after my brother's death, an FBI agent came to question me about him when I served as executive officer of the library at the U.S. Air Force Academy in Colorado.

(My eyes had slipped from 20/20 when I was working on my master's degree, effectively ending my fighter-pilot aspirations, meaning I fulfilled my three-year obligation stationed at the Air Force Academy.)

There wasn't anything I could tell the FBI agent, because I knew little to nothing of my brother's extracurricular activities, especially since 1,800 miles had separated us for three years. And the FBI agent played it very close to the vest, giving me vague hints about the reason for the investigation. But as part of the research for this book, I filed a Freedom of Information Act request with the FBI. What I learned from the 300-plus-page file was that my brother had been investigated for possible espionage involving the Soviet Union. The investigation had been triggered in the wake of one of the worst Cold War spy cases.

The case involved two army sergeants, Robert Lee Jones and James Mintkenbaugh, both of whom were convicted of espionage on behalf of the Soviet Union. From the highly redacted file, it appears some newspaper clippings found in my brother's office related to the spy scandal and letters to an acquaintance he had with someone who knew one of the two spies, put him under the FBI's microscope, especially after he committed suicide. While the investigation was excruciatingly detailed, the FBI's investigating office in the end concluded in a memo, dated August 6, 1965, to the FBI director:

> Background investigation of [Norbert] HEISE and the circumstances leading to his suicide has developed that he was a supreme egotist with financial goals he was unable to achieve. A philanderer by nature, he frequently nursed his ego with extramarital relationships. No information was developed that he was engaged in espionage... This matter does not warrant further investigation and is being closed.

I was stunned by the details that the FBI unearthed, but which — along with what little I knew -- completely justify the FBI's conclusion.

But in my search of his desk, I also found a manila envelope taped to the back of one of Norbert's desk drawers. It was filled with letters from a woman in Berlin named Ingeborg. The letters made it clear that this was not a fling, but rather appeared to be a very serious relationship that had gone on for some time. Ingeborg — whom he called his *Häschen* (little rabbit) in his letters — was a divorcee and the mother of a daughter for whom my brother seemed to care deeply. Indeed, I later saw letters from Norbert to Ingeborg in which he confessed his love for the child and hoped that one day he and Ingeborg would have a son whom he wanted to be very much like the son Simine and I had, Mark.

As fate would have it, I met Ingeborg in Berlin a few months later, after I left the Air Force. When I found out that my eyes were not good enough to become a fighter pilot, I set my sights on my second dream, to become a foreign correspondent. In those days, becoming a foreign correspondent usually meant years working for a news organization in the United States before being posted overseas. I decided to short-circuit the process.

Having a master's degree and being fluent in German, I was able to secure a one-year guest lectureship at Berlin's Free University. That was my base of operations and the source of a paycheck to support my family.

Almost immediately after arriving in Berlin in August 1965, I pounded on the door of every American news organization. Speaking German and having studied journalism, it seemed to me, should get me a job with someone. Sure enough, the Associated Press bureau had an opening on its American desk, and I was hired — at a modest wage, of course, given the frugality of the AP.

West Berlin was so different from when I had left it a dozen years earlier. Most of the rubble was gone although there were still skeletons of apartment houses here and there. But some modernistic building had gone up in the center of West Berlin. By and large, the people on the street were well dressed, and the stores were well stocked. With the exception of my students at the Free University, however, the older Germans were reluctant to speak about the Nazi era. And the police were not at all what I expected. While working for the AP, for example, I was assigned to cover the first major anti-Vietnam War demonstration. The demonstrators had chosen a Saturday to block the busiest intersection in West Berlin — the corner of *Kurfürstendamm* and *Joachimsthaler Strasse* — with a sit-down strike. Instead of the police contingent unsheathing their long batons, rolling out water cannons, much less firing tear gas, the officer in charge sat down in the middle of the intersection and started talking with the protest leaders. Eventually they agreed that the demonstrators could continue their sit-in for three hours and then, having made their point, disperse. At the agreed-on hour, the demonstrators stood up and left.

I met Ingeborg when I arrived ahead of my family in Berlin to find an apartment. The first time, she and I met at what was then one of West Berlin's best-known gathering spots, the

*Café Kranzle*r in the heart of Berlin. She turned out to be an attractive, charming woman. We speculated for hours — not only at the café but later over dinners at my and Simine's apartment — about why my brother took his life.

Simine, Ingeborg and I concluded – unaware of the FBI investigation -- that it had to be his disintegrating marriage (Ingeborg thought Norbert and his wife had separated, which was not true), his money troubles and what he felt was an unrequitable love for Ingeborg. After that initial meeting at the café, I went home and cried for the first time after my brother's death. She represented to me the glimmer of hope he should have pursued to live a happy life.

Had I known at the time the details in the FBI's investigative report, I doubt I would have shed even one tear. He even cheated repeatedly on his allegedly beloved *Häschen.* It's brutal to

find out – even after nearly a half century --
that your brother was utterly amoral.[10]

\*\*\*

I enjoyed my stint at the Free University,
especially since my light teaching load allowed
me to work full-time for the AP. And Berlin in
the mid-1960s was still a journalist's dream:
There was the story I broke for the AP about a
new Soviet missile-launching facility near the
Arctic circle, which was important because it
now allowed the Soviet Union to put satellites
into polar orbit as the United States had been
doing for some time. I worked on another story
about the crash of a Soviet reconnaissance jet
into a lake in the British sector, with all its
intelligence implications — the West did not
even have a picture of the jet — and political
ramifications during the Cold War. And there

---

[10] With the benefit of nearly 50 years hindsight and experience, I also think my
brother may have suffered from bipolar disease, which seems to run on my
mother's side of the family. One of my mother's sisters also committed suicide;
another was institutionalized for severe depression; and a cousin of mine on my
mother's side had to give up her effort to become a Lutheran pastor because of
her manic-depressive behavior.

were stories about the endless shootings and other incidents along the Wall.

But my dream to be a foreign correspondent ended in 1966, when a family emergency took me back to the States.

## 4: Getting *Das Haus* Back

**By J. Arthur Heise**

My father was never the same after my brother's death in 1965. My brother had been his favorite, as I was my mother's. After Norbert's death, my father became quieter, more introverted and smoked more.

In the fall of my second year in Berlin, I received an urgent call from my mother: My father had suffered a heart attack. Could I come back? She needed help coping with the situation. Being the only child left, I felt I had no choice. But that didn't make the choice any easier. The AP had just asked me to go to their main Eastern European bureau in Frankfurt for further training. Performing well there would have been a major step toward becoming a regular correspondent for the AP.

Instead, Simine and I headed back to Syracuse. My best journalist friend in Berlin, Joe Fleming, United Press International's Berlin bureau chief since the end of the war, seemed to know every American journalist of consequence. He sent a strong letter of recommendation to the managing editor of a major newspaper in New York City. The editor wrote back promptly with words to the effect that if Fleming thinks you're any good, you can count on a job with us. He was the managing editor of The New York Herald Tribune, which folded a few months later and with it my job opportunity.

So the hunt for a job not too far from Syracuse was on. I ended up with what was then The Buffalo *Evening News*. Buffalo was a far cry from Berlin, but a job was a job. Also, I had started some freelance work, one result of which was a book.[11] I didn't need a grumpy city editor to hector me to pursue a good story. However, the kind of nonfiction I was interested in would hardly make enough money to support my family. I had enjoyed teaching at the Free University, so I decided to pursue a university teaching career. It would allow me to continue writing about what

---

[11] J. Arthur Heise, *The Brass Factories: A Frank Appraisal of West Point, Annapolis and the Air Force Academy* (Washington, D.C.: Public Affairs Press, 1969).

interested me while also earning a decent salary. But that meant I needed academia's union card, the Ph.D. Since my writing interests at the time involved the U.S. military, I returned to my alma mater, Syracuse University, to earn a Ph.D. in its vaunted public administration program of the Maxwell School.

My three years there were the best time I ever spent at a university. When I worked on my undergraduate degree, I was always pressed for time between my studies and job while compressing a four-year program into three.

Now I had G.I. benefits, my wife found a teaching job, and every year at Maxwell I had either a fellowship or an assistantship. I now had the luxury of going to the library and if I saw a book of interest — though not necessarily related to my studies — I could find a quiet corner and read for hours. Or I could spend hours with faculty members discussing issues of importance to the field. I was in academic heaven.

But a very sad moment came in 1971. *Vati* had another heart attack, and this time he died instantly. He was 67.

We were in Teheran that summer, visiting my wife's family, when an emissary from the U.S. embassy knocked on the door at eight in the morning and told me of my father's death. I was back in Syracuse two days later. But after my father's burial, I took my mother with me to Teheran. That had been my wife's grandmother's idea. A totally different environment, she contended, would help my mother deal with her loss. She was right. Not only was my mother dazzled by the totally different culture she witnessed in Iran, but on her way back to the United States, she stopped in Germany to visit her two surviving sisters.

It was fortunate that I was attending the university in Syracuse at the time, so we could help my mother downsize to a comfortable apartment. And, of all things, I taught her, now in her 60s, how to drive. My father had never seen any need for her to handle a car.

The Syracuse days ended in early 1974, when I was recruited by a new school in the Florida state university system, Florida International University in Miami. FIU had just opened, and it had only 6,000 students when I arrived. Today it has about 50,000 students. I started out teaching in the public administration program, serving as its chair twice. But FIU was the wrong university for me to pursue my plan to combine teaching with my interest in writing. The school was growing rapidly, and my administrative duties were overwhelming.

I discovered I had management skills I never knew I possessed. One result was that in 1983, the provost asked me — because of my journalistic background — to see him about his "single biggest academic headache," the tiny department of communications. He asked me to chair it for a year and to recommend what should be done. What I found made the answer simple: Either shut the department down because it is so shoddy or, realizing that Miami is not only a significant media market but is also the gateway to the Americas, build a first-rate school of journalism that distinguishes itself through its focus on Latin America.

Since good deeds never go unpunished, the provost in time asked me to leave the public administration program and start building a fine school of journalism. I accepted the challenge.[12]

The focus on Latin America became a reality when we secured an $18 million, 10-year program, financed by the U.S. Agency for International Development, to strengthen journalism in Central America. As a result I was in San José, Costa Rica, on November 9, 1989. It had been a long day, starting with a breakfast meeting and ending with a long meeting over a late dinner. I had just returned to the San José Holiday Inn — then the city's

---

[12] After the school was accredited in record time, it became a free-standing unit — like the College of Business, for example — and I became its dean. During my time, six graduates won print journalism's highest honor, the Pulitzer Prize, in whole or as part of a team. Two did so twice. Also, the chair of the last accreditation team that visited while I was dean told the president of the university during the customary exit interview that what the accreditors found was a "program of national distinction."

best hotel despite the fact that one of its two elevators never seemed to work. Having been out of touch with the world all day, I turned on CNN but forgot to turn the sound up.

I was undressing to head for the shower when the fuzzy but colored picture on the screen caught my eye: It looked like the Berlin Wall was coming down. I turned up the sound and sat on the edge of my bed mesmerized for hours. The Wall couldn't be coming down, not in my lifetime. But it was. All those people who had been killed trying to get past the Wall had died in vain or spent years in jail for trying to get out of the German "Democratic" Republic.

It was almost impossible to grasp.

The event also meant something else. There was a house on the other side of the Wall, in Berlin-Karlshorst, that the Communists — first the Soviets, then the East German political elite — had had at their disposal for free for nearly five decades. That house had belonged to my parents, who had passed away, and now to me. Before the Wall came down, I had never given serious thought to getting the house back, because I was sure the Wall would never fall.

I would have certified anyone insane who would have told me that in my lifetime the Wall would topple and that the Union of Soviet Socialist Republics would soon go out of business.

That's also why I had made only a halfhearted attempt to catch a glimpse of the house when I worked for the AP and the Free University in Berlin in the 1960s. With an American passport that allowed me to go to East Berlin at any time, I drove to Karlshorst one day to see whether the *Sperrgebiet* still existed. From the side from which I approached Karlshorst, the restricted zone was very much in existence. The fences and guard towers sprouted signs that forbade entry even by foreign military — meaning service members of the three Western allies, who technically could go anywhere in Berlin. What I learned years later was that on the other side of the restricted zone — where my house sat — the fence had been moved back one block, allowing street access to my house, provided one knew a very circuitous route, which I didn't.

Right there in San José, Costa Rica, without consulting anybody, I made up my mind that, no matter what, I was going to get the house back. Little did I know what I would be up against during the next decade.

*Das Haus*

## 5. Fleeing to England, Hoping for USA

**By Melanie Kuhr**

I heard many stories about the house in Berlin-Karlshorst. My grandmother, Ruth Levy, spoke of the house with pride and longing. It was the home her father had built

She rarely talked about the events that led to her leaving her parents and the house behind. When she did speak of Germany, it was about the pre-Hitler Germany.

She would tell me about the Harz Mountains (*Ermsleben am Harz*), where she lived until age 10, later she and her parents moved to Berlin so her father could work for the family paint company -- presumably as a sales representative -- which was based in Pirna, near Dresden. Her father, Theodor, was one of six children. He grew up in the Harz Mountains, and his love of all things natural still runs in the family. My grandmother enjoyed her youth in Berlin, especially the gardens, parks and cultural amenities around the city. She was particularly proud that her grandfather, Mendel Hess, was court optician to the Duke of Anhalt and a talented singer.

Theodor Simonsohn built a house — *das Haus*

The topping-out celebration of *das Haus* in 1936.

— while he was in his 70s, which at that time was considered extremely old. Ruth, an only child, was 39 already — divorced and her former husband deceased — and was responsible for caring for my elderly great grandparents and Susanne, my mother. My great grandfather built the home as a haven — it offered both personal and financial security:

the first floor to live in, and a second-floor apartment for income.

*Om* often spoke of her love for her parents, the warmth of their home, and her beloved Minka, a whippet she later had to leave behind. (I called my grandmother *Om* because as a little girl, I couldn't pronounce *Oma*, the affectionate German term for grandmother.) Ruth married Max Levy in 1924, and in 1928 they had a daughter, my mother, Susanne, whom her family called Susie or *Sanchen*. *Om* told me she almost died in childbirth because my mother was so big; she was in labor for two days. Max stood 6 feet 4 inches, while my grandmother was a petite 5 foot 2. Always the prankster, she would get out a stepladder to kiss him at parties.

Max served in the German Army during World War I. In 1918, he won the Iron Cross, Second Class, for his bravery during the Second Battle of the Marne, in which the Allies' defeat of the Germans marked the beginning of the end of the war. He returned from the war with a serious heart ailment and died in 1933.

Max came from a German Jewish family that can be traced back five generations. My children and I are the last of Max's line; my mother, Susanne, was his only child, and none

**Max Levy won the Iron Cross Second Class in one of the decisive WWI battles.**

of his other siblings or their children survived the Holocaust.

*Om* showed me Max's portrait and the Iron Cross that she kept tightly wrapped in cotton so it would not rust.

For reasons I never knew, Ruth divorced Max "without fault" in 1932, a year before he died. Ruth always referred to herself as a widow, apparently in response to the stigma attached to divorce during those times. Ruth remained friendly with Max's mother and family, most of whom perished in the Nazi death camps. Ruth wore her wedding band until she died. She bequeathed the ring to me. *Om* told me she never remarried because she was afraid a new husband might not treat her Susie well. When I would visit her in her 90s, she would

**Theodor and Helene Simonsohn, who loved nature, are feeding tame squirrels in a Berlin park.**

laughingly say that "maybe this year I'll find a husband."

\*\*\*

Ruth and her parents, the Simonsohns, considered themselves Germans first and Jews second. The Simonsohns had assimilated into German society, as many Jews had before the Third Reich decimated the German Jewish communities. After *Kristallnacht* — known as the night of broken glass because of the Jewish store, home and synagogue windows that the Brownshirts smashed — the family decided it was time for Ruth to leave Germany. My grandmother's first choice was America. Many members of my great-grandmother's family had fled to Cincinnati in the early 1930s during Hitler's rise to power. Perhaps they were lucky, or perhaps they sensed where Germany's economic and political woes would lead. Ruth wrote her first letter to the Citizenship Council in Cincinnati in November 1939 — just two weeks after *Kristallnacht* — describing the unbearable living conditions in Germany and sought asylum for herself and Susanne. Gestapo agents had begun banging regularly on the door of *das Haus,* demanding payment and threatening to burn the house down. My great-grandfather paid them off to keep the family safe.

My grandmother's first choice was America. Many members of my great-grandmother's family had fled to Cincinnati in the early 1930s during Hitler's rise to power. Maybe it was just luck, or perhaps they sensed where Germany was heading. The United States at the time was reluctant to accept Jewish immigrants. Though Ruth's American cousins, Bernard and Louise Brockage, guaranteed that they would support Ruth and her daughter, they were still denied entry visas.

Having failed to obtain entry to the United States, she placed a small ad in a British newspaper with the help of a Jewish organization in Berlin:

> *German Jewess, 41, experienced with any household duties, good cooking, very fond of children, gardening work, knowledge of English, SEEKS SUITABLE POSITION. Ruth Levy, Berlin-Karlshorst, Neuwieder Strasse 55.*

This is what it had come to. This was a woman who had studied French, English and Italian; a woman who warmed up horses at the Berlin-Karlshorst track in the mornings; a woman who, as Ruth Salden, had performed for the legendary theatrical and film director Max Reinhardt on Berlin stages in the Twenties. This was a woman who, despite all the misery she had experienced, was full of grace, kindness, love and a contagious *joie de vivre* that she maintained her entire life..

But as the persecution of Jews grew worse and worse, she knew she had to get out of the country. Her parents became ever more fearful and urged her and Susie to flee.

And she succeeded, although she was not allowed by the Third Reich to take her daughter her own passage out of Germany, she would have no chance of saving her Susie from certain death at the hands of the Nazis. Fortunately,

Ruth was offered a position as housekeeper at

**Ruth Levy, 72 when this photo was taken , was the daughter of Theodor and Helene Simonsohn, and was Melanie's grandmother — her *Om*.**

the Park Farm, a large dairy farm, in Tewksbury, England. The owners, Madge and Roger Troughton, whose family had owned the farm for 500 years, hired her. She started taking care of the main house there in February 1939. It was a large, two-story brick house that was often cold and damp until my grandmother started and stoked the fireplace every morning at five. Among the many papers she left behind I found a daily journal that she kept while working at the dairy farm.

**Ruth Levy Simonsohn, right, and her daughter Susanne, in a photo likely taken shortly before Ruth fled to England.**

It included everything from instructions on the daily routine spelled out by Mrs. Troughton to a collection of recipes the five Troughton boys liked best. It is so detailed that, when I reread it, I feel as if I were in that cold kitchen with *Om* as she lighted the fire.

For the first five months, however, her main concern was how to get her daughter out of Germany. The situation kept getting worse: Jewish children were harassed daily and forced

94

to wear a yellow Star of David. They had to add either "Sarah" or "Israel" to their given name, and were no longer allowed to attend public school, swim in the community pools, dine or shop in non-Jewish establishments or attend Jewish services.

The Nazis limited Ruth's ability to communicate with Susanne. Until 1939, Germany allowed mail between German Jewish children and their family members outside the country. But once the war began, those remaining in Germany were allowed to send and receive only 25-word "letters" written by family and delivered by the Red Cross.

My mother always bore the marks of her early childhood in Nazi Germany — always keeping quiet, maintaining a low profile and understanding what it meant to be different. For example, when I was growing up in Cincinnati — "the gateway to the South" —- in the 1960s, segregation and the civil rights struggle were part of the everyday experience.

Despite the skeptical glances of neighbors and passersby, my mother insisted on serving lunch on the porch to the African-American workers Dad brought home to work on the pool or in the yard, and she alone drove them to the bus stop at day's end. Sometimes words were exchanged in the driveway when mother would not accept a "no ma'am." She brushed away the concerns of the workers themselves and insisted they get inside her station wagon; she was driving them to the bus. On Fridays, beer was shared at the end of the workday. My mother knew what it felt like to be a minority segregated from the majority, and she had an empathetic understanding of what it meant to be a second-class citizen, born into a despised minority and legally discriminated against by a hate-filled majority.

My mother often said to me if it were not for the bravery of my grandmother Ruth, both she and I would not be on this Earth. Ruth knew what was at risk if she did not leave Germany and find a way to bring her daughter out. By 1939, members of the family had been sent to labor camps. My mother knew she was fortunate to have a brave mother who would do whatever it took to get her out of Nazi Germany.

Most countries would not accept Jews seeking to flee Germany at this point, but the British government soon after *Kristallnacht* agreed to allow the entry of up to 10,000[13] Jewish and other threatened children from Germany, Austria, Poland and Czechoslovakia.[14]

In contrast, the U.S. Congress let a bill to admit 20,000 children die in committee because admitting children without their parents was "contrary to the laws of God."[15]

An estimated 1.5 million children died in the Holocaust.

My mother Susanne was one of the fortunate 10,000. Ruth was advised on April 21, 1939, that Susie was on the waiting list for the Kindertransport to Britain.

---

[13] United States Holocaust Memorial Museum, Holocaust Encyclopedia, *Kindertransport, 1938-45*

[14] This section draws extensively on Mark Jonathan Harris, *Into the Arms of Strangers: Stories of the Kindertransport;* a documentary, 2000. See also Susanne Heim, "Immigration Policy and Forced Immigration from Germany: The Situation of Jewish Children (1933-1945," *Children and the Holocaust, Symposium Presentation* (U.S. Holocaust Memorial Center: Center for Advanced Holocaust Studies 2004) 10.

[15] *Ibid.*

**Susanne in front of *das Haus* just before she fled to England.**

She was more fortunate than the others among those 10,000, because they had to leave their parents behind in Germany, most of whom eventually perished in the camps. Susanne's mother was waiting for her in England.

Some among the 9,000 to 10,000 children, especially the older ones, were difficult to place with British families. While many of the children were placed in happy homes, some ended up bouncing from home to home, and others stayed in youth hostels and unused summer camps.

My mother was forever grateful to the English, and many times lamented leaving England, as the life there was more suitable to her than the American lifestyle.

Ruth and Susanne were finally reunited in Southampton in June 1939, when Susie's Kindertransport arrived. My mother ended up attending the Naunton Park School in Cheltenham, five miles from the dairy farm where Ruth worked. So during the week, my mother stayed with Miss Constance Allen, a nurse, who lived in Cheltenham. But on the weekends, Mom would join her mother at the farm. (Miss Allen and my mother stayed in touch until my mother's death in 1994.)

Life for Ruth and Susanne was far from perfect, but they were together, and they were alive. They lived for news that Theodor and Helene Simonsohn were okay and prayed for their safety. At first, there were letters and parcels -- and then nothing.

When Susanne left Germany, Theodor and Helene packed her trunk full of clothes, silver pieces, jewelry, rolled art work and the like, The Nazis allowed Jewish citizens to take only 10 German marks in cash when they left the country. I was told Susanne was instructed to keep the trunk locked, and fortunately it made its way to England; for many years they sold off some of those pieces to survive.

For a year, they settled into their new lives in England, but soon there was fear and disruption again when England decided to intern many German aliens. My grandmother was arrested at the farm and taken to Cheltenham, where she gathered my mother from school. They were sent to the Women's Internment Camp at Port St. Mary on the Isle of Man from June 1940 to February 1941 with thousands of other "resident aliens" in England. Living conditions there were abysmal. Yams were the staple of their diet. My mother was malnourished and contracted rickets; my grandmother came down with scarlet fever, which, poorly treated, left her partially deaf. The damage to her hearing was not correctible with hearing aids, and she lived with a rumbling in her ears for the rest of her life.

When Ruth and Susanne were released from internment in 1941, they returned to Cheltenham for the rest of the war, with Ruth working as a domestic in several households. My mother resumed her grade-school education and then attended North Gloucestershire Technical College until age 17. Once the war was over, my grandmother told me, the British lifted the restrictions on aliens that had prohibited them from taking any jobs other that serving as household help. My grandmother secured various jobs, including that of secretary with the Cheltenham & Gloucester Building Society.

But my grandmother's top priority was to get out of Europe and to come to the United States. She again wrote to the U.S. Citizenship Council with the guarantee of her Cincinnati cousins.

There was a complication, however. Toward the end of the war, my mother had fallen in love with a young Polish soldier named Roman Posnanski. She met him at one of the many weekend dances she attended in Cheltenham, where he was stationed along with soldiers from all of the Allied nations. My grandmother — who, despite her diminutive appearance, could be very determined, even feisty — would have none of it. They were going to the United States. She had had enough of Europe! And on July 11, 1947, they left England via South Hampton and sailed to New York.

**Susanne and her Polish soldier boyfriend**

Similar to what happened to Art Heise's family, my grandmother's cousin in Cincinnati thought that Ruth and Susanne would be good household help in their modest Indian Hill home in exchange for room and board. Ruth, the very proper but iron-willed person she was, did not like that idea at all. As far as she was concerned, they had not lost everything to become household workers for her own family. It was an insult *Om* never forgave, and we were never in touch again with the Brockage family. Members of the Brockage family still reside in Cincinnati, and the sons own a well-known landscaping firm.

Ruth found a secretarial position with the United Methodist Church. She worked there until retirement and came to live with my parents and me when I was born in 1961. My mother found a job with the Hebrew Union College, which ordains Reform rabbis still today. Seeking to make more money, she applied for a position with International Harvester's office in Cincinnati. The interview went well, but the district manager, her future boss, told her he would have to poll the other office employees to see how they felt about having a Jewess in their workplace. Such was Southern Ohio in the Fifties. But she was approved and worked for International Harvester until she married my father, Alvin Kuhr, in 1961. Only during the first year of their marriage did grandmother live in her own apartment, and as soon as I was born in 1961, she came to live with us.

My mother, Susanne, made many friends during her work years and traveled with them to explore New York, Chicago, San Francisco and Florida. She even found time to be the president of the opera star Roberta Peters's fan club in Cincinnati.

Susanne was a young woman whose youth was stolen, and for the first time in 19 years she could enjoy acceptance and freedom in her new country.

Ruth and Susanne found a third-story apartment on Mitchell Avenue in Cincinnati. They befriended the family below, and Susanne often babysat a little boy named Jimmy Levine. Little Jimmy grew up to become James Levine, the internationally renowned conductor of the New York Metropolitan Opera. My mother and grandmother shared his family's love for music, particularly opera. Indeed, much of their social life revolved around the opera, and Susanne sometimes took roles as an extra. When Levine would conduct in Cincinnati, they would never miss the performance.

One day, while checking out available real estate, Susanne met Alvin Kuhr, the man who would become my father. (Born Abraham Isaac, he Americanized his name in the Thirties.)

His was an interesting story. Known as Al, he survived a hard life in a hard world and, as a result, became a very hard person. Sadly, although he was married four times and fathered three children, his life ended in the way he most feared — alone.

My dad was born in Cincinnati in 1910 to Gerson and Bella Kuhr, who immigrated to the United States at the turn of the 20th century from Russia. Al's father was a machinist for a lock company in Cincinnati, and Bella was a seamstress. A sister, Lena, was born after Al, but she died in infancy. Al's mother suffered from depression after the death of the child, and she went back to Russia and took little 5-year-old Alvin with her. More than depression drove Bella back to Russia; while her doctor told her to go back to her family in Russia to recover, it was really to help her get away from Gerson. He was harsh and abusive to his young wife, as he was later to his son Alvin.

While they were in her homeland, WWI broke out. The borders closed, and for the next seven years, Al was trapped with his mother and her family in a small house in a rural *shtetl*. He recalled that the home had dirt floors, and when it was terribly cold outside, they would bring the cow and other animals into the kitchen.

The kitchen was also a place of safety because his *Zaide* (grandfather in Yiddish) had dug out a space in the mud walls behind the oven, where he hid Bella and little Alvin when the Russian soldiers came through, raping and pillaging, on their way to the front.

My Dad spoke fondly of his Russian *Zaide,* who raised him from age 5 to 13. His grandfather called him his Kaddish, since he was the only boy and thus the only one who could recite the Kaddish — the Jewish prayer of mourning — upon his death.

Once the war ended, Bella tried to get papers for her and her son from the U.S. consulate to secure passage back to the United States.. Russia was a place of ever-increasing danger for Jews; pogroms were now a regular occurrence. *Zaide* found a local who would smuggle Bella and Alvin across the border in a horse-drawn sleigh. My father told us many times about the wolves, the cold and the fear he encountered lying under straw and blankets on the sleigh as they traveled through the night. What country they reached I don't know, but eventually they escaped Russia, located a U.S. consulate and secured passage home.

Husband and wife had been separated for seven years. Bella did not want to return to Cincinnati; she wanted to remain in New York City with cousins. But there was a phone call from Gerson in which he insisted she come back to Cincinnati, and she did as she was told. She returned to the harsh man who had beaten her and her young son. They resumed life as a family, and two more children were born after Bella's return from Russia.

But Alvin was never accepted back into his father's life; he was a different boy now, one who spoke only Russian and Yiddish, one raised by his beloved Russian *Zaide.* Moreover, Gerson was jealous of the close relationship between Alvin and his mother.

He had little patience for an adolescent whom he saw as a stranger. Gerson beat his son physically and badgered him emotionally. Before long, my Dad was sleeping on couches in the homes of family members. Not long after my Dad turned 16 but was still in the eighth grade, his father held open the door to the house and told Alvin to go out into the world and "find your place."

Alvin was dismissed like a stray dog, sent out into the world before the age of 16 to fend for himself. Having lost his families in Russia and

Cincinnati, my Dad hopped on a rail car and headed to California in 1926.

One problem he had to overcome was that he could speak only Russian, Yiddish and broken English. But like Art, he was determined to learn to speak English without a trace of an accent. He traveled around the country, surviving as a hobo, but learning to speak the language fluently. These experiences shaped his life. He was a survivor, too, although his experiences — unlike Ruth's and Susanne's — made him harsh.

Suffering emotional and physical abuse at a young age can do that to a person. The difference between Al's response to living in a hard world and Ruth and Susanne's may rest in the fact that Al's tormentor was his father. Ruth and young Susanne were persecuted by their society, but as long as they were together they were home.

Handsome and 6-foot-2, with cold blue eyes, dark hair and an athletic build, he spent several years in Los Angeles as an escort to older wealthy women, taxi driver, movie extra and entrepreneur. During his time in Los Angeles, his parents had two more children, Edith and Alfred. A visiting friend from Cincinnati informed Alvin that his family's finances had not improved and that they did not have proper food or clothing. He returned to Cincinnati to help his mother; he and his father still did not get along.

So Alvin Kuhr, my Dad, started making a living in the rag business; when World War II started, he moved into the scrap metal business. Although he had only an eighth-grade education, he was charismatic, energetic, adept at mathematics and had a keen business sense. He soon became a homebuilder and, ultimately, a prominent real estate developer in Ohio and later in South Florida.

According to my mother, they met at one of his construction sites. She and my grandmother Ruth spent an occasional Sunday looking at open houses and new developments. They were upstairs in one of the townhouses Alvin was building in a northern suburb of Cincinnati, a neighborhood he developed. A white Cadillac convertible with a red leather interior pulled up and this tall distinguished-looking man got out. My mother, who was a pretty young woman with dark brown eyes, but also very reserved, said to my grandmother, "Hurry up, let's go. The owner is here."

By that time, Alvin Kuhr was coming up the stairs. My Dad was an outgoing man who never met a stranger. He started talking to the two women and before long, fascinated with her dark good looks and accent, he asked Susanne for her telephone number.

My grandmother was furious because Alvin was much older than Susanne. But they dated, and they married in 1961, the year I was born. Previously married, widowed and already a grandfather, my father was 18 years older than my mother, who was 33 at the time. Initially, they had a warm relationship. My father built a beautiful four-bedroom house for us that I loved because it accommodated not only me and my parents, but also my *Om,* who had one wing of the house. And virtually unheard-of in those days in Ohio, the house had a swimming

**Melanie's parents, Alvin and Susanne Kuhr.**

pool. Situated on a one-acre lot, it gave my mother and grandmother ample space to pursue their favorite hobby, gardening. And a beautiful garden — with roses, sunflowers and an ornamental pond — they created. When I was young, my *Om* was my best friend and constant playmate. But her time in Nazi Germany and wartime England left her sometimes fearful and overly protective. For example, when my parents were away, *Om,* at first hint of dusk, would rush around the house and close all the shades and curtains. She insisted on having a deadbolt installed on my bedroom door. When my parents traveled and we were alone, she would bolt my bedroom door and we would sleep together in my room. She was anxious if I wore the diamond Star of David necklace that my one of father's friends had given me. I did not understand...

**Oil painting of Theodor Simonsohn**

Hanging on the wall of her bedroom were two oil paintings, one of my great-grandfather, Theodor, the other of my great-grandmother, Helene. My great-grandfather wears a starched collar and a tie with a beautiful pin — which *Om* later wore as a ring and I do now — with a stern expression; my great-grandmother wears a brocade dress with a white insert at the neck and a slight smile on her face. How my grandmother got those pictures out of Germany remains a mystery. The only explanation is that she took the paintings out of their frames, rolled them up and brought them out of Germany in the steamer trunk that accompanied Susanne to England and had them reframed.

**Oil painting of Helene Simonsohn.**

Today they occupy a prominent place in my home to remind me and my three children — Allison, Andrew and Alexander — of their forebears. Not a person walks into my home who does not comment on the striking couple; many are shocked to learn that I am the child of Holocaust survivors and that my children are only three generations removed from Holocaust victims.

The question the pictures raise, of course, is why my great-grandparents did not try to escape Germany.

They were in their mid-70s and Theodor was infirm. Perhaps they, like many, hoped they could ride out the scourge of the Third Reich. They may have hoped time would be their friend. I only know some limited facts about Theodor and Helene: I know that Helene — her maiden name was Hess — was born in Bernburg, Germany, to one of three children of Mendel Hess and Berta Mueller. She married her distant cousin Theodor Simonsohn in November 1893 at the age of 29 and moved to the Harz Mountains. Helene's brother Gustav founded a chemical factory near Dresden, in 1895. Theodor went to work for Gustav as his agent in Berlin a couple of years later.

(Art speculates that that is perhaps how Theodor knew Art's father, whose factory used significant qualities of varnish and paint for the electrical equipment he built and repaired.)

Neither my mother nor grandmother ever spoke of why the Simonsohns did not attempt to leave

Germany. Indeed, they rarely spoke of the Nazi era. The Germany they remembered and talked about fondly were the pre-Hitler years. My speculation is that the answer is twofold. First, the Simonsohns' ages. At the time of *Kristallnacht*, my great-grandmother was 74, my great grandfather, 72. How could they start over in a foreign land at that age, even if there was one that would accept them? Besides, my grandfather was not in the best of health, constantly requiring a urinary catheter.

And they were Germans first. This was their country and had been for generations. They simply could not believe that the darkness that was enveloping them tighter every day could last, much less get worse. Like many, they probably hoped that they could wait out the "troubles," that eventually they would welcome their beloved Ruth and Susanne back home, that time would be their friend.

It was not.

## 6. Melanie: A World Away

**By Melanie Kuhr**

My early years could not have been more different from my mother's. I had a lovely home, lived in a Jewish community where I did not feel different or afraid of being Jewish. My days were filled with swimming, skating, tennis, school, camp, love, fun, family and lots of neighborhood friends.

My extended family lived nearby, and I have fond memories of celebrating holidays and birthdays together. I enjoyed lots of attention, spoiled by my *Om,* our housekeeper, Mattie, and my Mom. Our home had plenty of land for gardens, an ornamental pond and a swimming pool. Pool parties and holidays at my house were the social center of our family. Later we spent winters in a house in Fort Lauderdale, Florida, also built by my father.

But my early years also could not have been more unusual. Because my father was the

**Three generations of Simonsohns: Susanne Kuhr, left, Melanie Kuhr, center, Ruth Levy, right.**

widowed father of two children, who in turn had five children, I was an aunt the day I was born. I grew up with my five nieces and nephews as though we were siblings. My two half-brothers from my father's first marriage, Don and Dick, were more than 20 years my senior.

\*\*\*

Alvin Kuhr had a history of philandering; he felt he was entitled. And he was a tyrant at home.

When he came home from work, it was like a blast of cold bitter wind sweeping into the house. During the day, everyone was happy; when he arrived home around seven o'clock, we all walked on eggshells. Anything he perceived as critical of him enraged him.

One night the table — food, dishes and all — went flying across the kitchen. I remember seeing the food splattered against the wall.

Once when I was about 9, I said something to him in the car while we were driving down Commercial Boulevard in Fort Lauderdale that he felt was an insult, and he told me to get out of the car. My mother was crying in the front seat, and I remember standing on the street and watching my parents drive away. They did come back, but whether it was five minutes or five hours I don't remember. After that, I knew better than to express my thoughts.

My Dad was a sociopath. You never knew who would walk in the door. He was angry and mean, and he focused his cruelty on those he loved or who needed him the most. There was one way: the Al Kuhr way. And if you did not follow his path, there was a price to pay, physically and mentally.

Somehow I grew up to be unafraid of my Dad. I learned early on to just go with it and "yes, sir" him and keep my feelings to myself. But contempt grew in my heart, and I loathed the way he treated my *Om* and my mother. After I left for college, I rarely returned home, only to visit for a weekend, to see my Mom and *Om*. But it was painful to see them living in fear.

Alvin Kuhr was a man of great contradictions. I saw him buy meals for the poor who scavenged from his scrap yard. One of his trusted friends was the Catholic monsignor from the neighborhood he grew up in. My Dad did a lot to help many a family, but he did not show the same grace to his own family.

That's why my grandmother left everything to me, skipping over my mother, because she knew if she left her estate, including the Karlshorst house, to my mother, it would all disappear into Alvin's pocket.

Both of my parents were survivors; while their hardships were different they experienced many of the same things: loss, fear, persecution, and deprivation. And how those early experiences affected their lives could not have played out more differently. My mother looked for the beauty in all things and viewed life as a glass half full; my Dad always saw the beastly side and tended to view life as a glass half empty.

Just as I graduated from high school, my father, who was 69 at the time, had a severe heart attack. Despite my feelings about him, I got cold feet about going to college too far from home.

So, instead of the University of Denver, I decided to go to the 1,400-student Marietta College in Ohio. It was only a three and a half hour drive from home. My best friend, Robin, had begged me to apply with her. Robin's compelling reason? The ratio of men to women was three to one, and she was going to college to earn a "Mrs." That wasn't something that appealed to me at the time.

Marietta proved to be a great place for me to grow independent of my family. I came into my own in college. I continued playing tennis, became the president of my sorority, Sigma Kappa, and vice president of the student body. Initially, I majored in psychology, but my Dad reminded me that one day I would need to earn a living. As a result, I added a business major and earned a degree in industrial labor relations, a move that would help me land my first job after graduation. And I met my future husband, Eric Murphy, my college sweetheart.

\*\*\*

Well before I went to college, two events occurred that I will never forget. The first happened in 1974, when my mother took me back to England to visit Cheltenham, where she had spent the war years as a child. The large, cold brick house was exactly as she remembered it. So was the dairy farm that was now managed by one of the sons of Roger and Madge Troughton. Years earlier, my mother and Dad visited England, and my mother was treated like royalty. According to the *Gloucestershire Echo,* my mother said, "When I first arrived, speaking not a word of English, I was surrounded by girls who had never seen a foreigner before and bombarded me with questions I couldn't understand."

She visited with the mayor of Cheltenham and the headmaster of the Naunton Park School she had attended. She told the headmaster of the school that she wished she could send her 5-year-old daughter to a school like Naunton Park. "My little girl [Melanie] could do with some English discipline," she added, laughing.

During this trip, it occurred to me for the first time that my mother was a remarkably strong and determined person. I felt how far away her childhood was, and I began to understand what it meant to be a child of the Holocaust.

The other occurred in 1971. Through the Jewish Refugees Committee, my *Om* had reconnected with a cousin, Horst Katz, who now lived in Brazil. He and his family had lived in Berlin during the Nazi years. Horst's parents were deported, and he and his sister, Edith, were left behind. Somehow Horst and Edith survived. Horst made his way to a German port, sneaked aboard a ship and hid in the cargo hold. He had no idea where the ship was going. After weeks of scraping by on whatever he could find, he found himself in Brazil. Edith found her way to Australia, where she lived out her life.

Horst's first job was as a miner in a gemstone mine. As the years went by, he managed to become the owner of that and several other gemstone mines. When my family and I visited him and his family in 1970, he lived in a luxurious multi-level home right on the Copacabana promenade, Rio de Janeiro's famous beach boulevard. My mother and grandmother could speak to Horst in German, but his children didn't speak a word of English and I no Portuguese.

We had a great time, nevertheless, playing on the beach, visiting their mountain home, and experiencing New Year's celebrations Rio style. It was a city of extremes: the beauty and excess of Copacabana and then my father carrying me on his shoulders so the lepers and beggars in the Rio streets could not touch my white blonde hair, which they had never seen. I still remember how comforting it was to see Coca-Cola — a touch of home — sold on the beach. And Horst showered my mother and grandmother with a variety of gems that I still have to this day, reminding me of a wonderful month in Rio. But more important, I saw how Horst had not only survived but thrived. Through many hardships, the commitment to his family never wavered. It impressed me to see his true joy in seeing *Om* again; both of them clearly survived through steely determination. It does not come to me by chance.

***

 My father, Alvin Kuhr, had a large family, two sons by his first wife and five grandchildren. We regularly observed the various Jewish holidays, something my Mom and *Om* had never done. Judaism was not central to their life, since they had not been free to experience Jewish life in Nazi Germany. Indeed, following the German tradition, my *Om* would still have a Christian advent calendar and a Christmas tree in her room, much to my delight and perhaps my father's chagrin.

But now, surrounded by a large Jewish family, *Om,* at age 63, and my mother, at 32, were thrust into Judaism. My mother had to learn the rituals as though she had never been exposed to the religion. Like my nieces and nephews, I attended Sunday religious school at a Reform synagogue. I was confirmed at 16 but never became a Bat Mitzvah. Mother, *Om* and Mattie, our housekeeper, would prepare huge Holy Day celebrations and Shabbat dinners for my family, including my half-brothers, their five children, their wives and the wives' parents. We did go to temple on the High Holy Days and lighted the Shabbat candles on Friday night. Even though my Dad was raised in an Orthodox home and maintained an observant Jewish life with his first wife, my family was what I would call "Jewish lite." I knew I was Jewish, though I'm not sure I knew what that meant. But it was certainly a part of my identity. I don't think of my mother and grandmother as observant Jews, but they believed in God, seeing him reflected in nature and life's beauty. They were connected to God through the flowers and the birds — not through studying Torah or keeping kosher.

My Jewish education started in kindergarten with my consecration, and later I was confirmed and enjoyed my friends and study at Isaac M. Wise Temple on Plum Street. I stuck with "Sunday school" until my high school graduation. My confirmation class dedicated our service to family members who perished or suffered during the Shoah, the Holocaust.

I really began to ask questions and wanted to know more about my Mom's and grandmother's experiences. It was difficult for my Mom to recall details; she was a young girl when she left Germany. She also was a very reserved person and speaking about herself was uncomfortable for her. I think I am outspoken and assertive because I communicated for both of us as I was growing up.

My *Om* and mother both lived in the present, so they rarely talked about that period. They did not live their lives with anger, hatred or resentment. They focused on the positive, which was a wonderful model for not only me but also for everyone who befriended them. *Om's* focus was on the pre-Hitler Germany of which she was very fond.

My grandmother believed that as long as there are Jews on the Earth, they would be persecuted. The Jews had been persecuted for five millennia. She did not know why, especially since Judaism is not a proselytizing religion, and the basic tenet is *tikkun olam* — Hebrew for "healing the world."

I admired and adored my *Om*, but I had a different view of being Jewish. I decided to give the gift of Judaism to my children, despite the fact that I had married outside the faith. I came to feel that being Jewish is a blessing, not a curse. My *Om* thought I should use the opportunity of marrying a non-Jew to allow my children the peace of not being Jews. I felt that if I didn't raise my children as Jews, I would be betraying my great-grandparents and my heritage. It would have meant furthering Hitler's vision of a world without Jews. A core value I've lived by — and one that's certainly grounded in my heritage — is that doing the right thing is not always the easy thing. And just maybe being Jewish is so special that, even after a history of persecution, the Jewish people are still able to thrive. Even out of the Holocaust came something wondrous — the State of Israel.

My eventual decision to work with Art related to the recovery of the house in Berlin-Karlshorst was undergirded by my Jewish soul. I felt compelled to finish the work my *Om* had started in the 1950s when she first submitted a claim for restitution, ensuring that my family's memory would be preserved and honored. Since their voices were never heard, I put a lot of thought and heart into every decision I made in the journey with Art. Sometimes he got angry and frustrated when I appeared unresponsive, but the decisions were not only financial and contractual. It was a personal journey. I needed to reconcile myself with my heritage. I felt my memories of Ruth and Susanne would guide me to do the right thing.

\*\*\*

As the years went by, our life in Cincinnati began to fray. My father was 73 and wanted to retire — again. He had retired a couple of times before, but became bored and returned to work.

But this time my father was determined to retire in Florida. My mother and grandmother were vehemently opposed to such a move; Cincinnati was home for 35 years and they had lovingly created the gardens at my home for 23 years. Since I had left home to go to college, my *Om* was no longer needed as my keeper, as far as my father was concerned. He wanted my grandmother out of the house.

He prevailed, of course, about heading to Florida. In 1983, we moved to a much smaller house in Tamarac, just north of Miami. While the new house was considerably smaller than the Ohio house, it was roomy enough to accommodate my grandmother in her own room. My mother had no intention of leaving her mother in Cincinnati; aside from the time in 1939, they had never been apart.

They made the best of South Florida. They enjoyed the beaches and the arts, and they made friends in their Woodlands neighborhood. My mother became very active in the local chapters of B'nai B'rith and Hadassah.

But then tragedy and joy struck nearly simultaneously. My mother was diagnosed with bone cancer in 1989, just as I learned I was pregnant with Allison, my first child.

My mother's illness was the first tragedy I'd experienced in what had been a relatively perfect life — a world away from the one my mother grew up in. Mom battled, received a bone transplant and extended her life four years. She remained confident she would conquer the disease, as she limped along with her ever-present crutch. She didn't. She died in 1994 at age 65.

My grandmother's will to live evaporated when she realized her *Sanchen* (as she always called her beloved Susie) was dying.

She asked me what would become of her. I lived in Plano, Texas, at the time. I was a 33-year-old with a 4-year-old daughter and a responsible job at Ross Perot's Electronic Data Systems (EDS). *Om* had lived with my parents from the day I was born in 1961 until her death in 1994. *Om* was my loving grandmother, my second mother, playmate, protector and disciplinarian.

But joining me in Texas was simply not in her plan, and she stopped eating. My *Om* died March 25, 1994, less than a month shy of her 97th birthday. I went to Cincinnati to bury my *Om* while my Mom underwent her last surgery at Jackson Memorial Hospital in Miami. I operated on autopilot.

Twelve weeks later, my half-brother Don phoned me in the middle of the night to tell me my Mom was also gone.

All I remember from that time is watching the O.J. Simpson spectacle unfold as I waited standby in Fort Lauderdale for a flight to take my Mom's remains back to Cincinnati. *Om* and my mother chose their final resting place in the Jewish section of a Cincinnati cemetery, side by side on a hillside, overlooking trees where birds and squirrels abound. My mother wanted pieces of stone from Masada that she had collected on a trip to Israel in the 1970s included in her casket. Perhaps through it all she still clung to her connection to our forebears Abraham, Isaac, Jacob, Sarah, Rebekah, Leah and Rachel.

# 7: *Das Haus* Intervenes

**By Melanie Kuhr**

The deaths of my Mom and my *Om* so close together in 1994 were devastating. What helped me bear the grief were my hectic and evolving career and raising Allison. I now also had a lot of responsibility with my Dad; he was 85 and a widower for the second time. He never did well on his own; he was a man of many needs. When my mother was in the hospice, I remember him crying in her room, not for her but for him. He was crying about what was to become of him, an old man without a wife to take care of him.

In the 11 years before my mother and grandmother's deaths, I was independent and glad to be away from the tensions in Cincinnati. I never had any intention of staying there.

What helped me gain that independence was that, through Marietta College, I found a career that I came to enjoy. One of the graduates of my alma mater was the chief executive of

Procter & Gamble. As a result, P & G did a lot of recruiting at Marietta College. I was hired in 1983 as a sales management trainee, assigned to the Pittsburgh area. I accepted that job because my future husband, who had studied petroleum engineering, was planning to get a job with the Gulf Oil Company, then headquartered in Pittsburgh.

Being a sales representative turned out to be a challenge in an area where one steel company after another was collapsing or moving overseas. It was a great learning experience about an America that I had never seen. When I called on distributors and grocers in the Rust Belt and tried to sell them disposable diapers, I was greeted with incredulity. People are eating dog food, I was told; who can afford disposable diapers?

Eric Murphy and I were married in 1984 in Cincinnati's Isaac M. Wise Temple. Our grand plan to work together in the same town, Pittsburgh, went out the window when Gulf Oil shut its doors two weeks before Eric graduated.

He found a position, but it was in Dallas, Texas. I followed him to Dallas. While waiting for a sales territory to open with P&G, I was hired as a recruiter for Ross Perot's EDS, just after it was taken over by General Motors. It was a perfect job; recruiting used my college education and the sales experience I had gained with P&G in Pittsburgh.

I was career-minded and ambitious. By the time I was 33, I was managing 240 people. In the 10 years I was with EDS, I experienced professional success in the human relations field. I kept getting promoted and made good money. I was moved to corporate headquarters and became a vice president. My goal was to become a division president, and I was on that track.

In 1990, I had my first child, Allison. She kept complaining that she did not want to be a "lonely" child. So in 1997, I had our second child, Andrew. After a maternity leave, I went back to work at a time when EDS was undergoing major changes. I was assigned to a special project that involved a great deal of travel. Eric's job also required constant travel. Our jobs took both of us all over the world, away from our children, who were looked after by a South African au pair.

*** 

During this hectic time, both personally and professionally, another complexity was about to enter my life.

I was at an EDS/GM plant in Rüsselsheim, Germany, and Eric was in Italy. I called the au pair in Dallas and she told me that the evening before she had been at an event at the Stark Club and she had kissed the basketball star Dennis Rodman.

That was my epiphany. What am I doing? I'm in Germany and Daddy is in Italy and we have left the children at home with an au pair who is out kissing Dennis Rodman. What are we doing?

When Eric and I were back in the States, we had a long conversation about someone having to be a parent at home. Now financially able to do so, I decided to stay at home until Andrew was in kindergarten. Then we had a surprise when Alexander came along in 2000.

Meanwhile, Eric's job took him away from home even more frequently, as he pursued a successful career in business information technology.

We had moved so many times — Dallas to Washington, back to Dallas, back to Washington, then to Chicago, back to Dallas, and the moving was not over yet....

In the midst of all this — moving about the country, dealing with a challenging job and raising a family — one evening in the fall of 1997 the telephone rang in my little second-floor hideaway.

Someone named Art Heise wanted to talk to me about a house in Berlin-Karlshorst. I knew immediately what house he was speaking about.

I felt scared. I did not want anything to do with something as sickening as the ugly stories the house brought to my mind.

## 8: The Junkyard Dog

**By J. Arthur Heise**

Once I had returned to Miami from Costa Rica, the recovery of the house in Berlin slid to the back burner for a while, given how busy I was with the constant travel to Central and South America, not to mention the task of building and running a school of journalism.

It moved to the front burner when I received a disturbing call from a friend of my late parents who warned me that the new government of the unified Germany had set a deadline for filing claims for property that had been taken over by the East German government. She called me because she knew the Russians in 1945 had thrown my parents out of the house they owned in East Berlin. She also told me that there was a representative of a German law firm making the rounds in Syracuse proselytizing German-Americans, especially German-American Jews, who had property that had been expropriated.

141

She gave me his number, and I called the law firm's roving representative. He told me he was not actually an attorney, but an agent for the law firm. He was looking for owners of real estate in the former East Germany. He said the law firm would charge $350 to file a claim on my behalf. I paid, and the Wiesbaden-based firm filed my claim in December 1990 — before the deadline.

The first thing the lawyers sent me were copies of forms filled out by other claimants of the property. One of the first was the Conference on Jewish Material Claims Against Germany, Inc., which had offices in Berlin. The Conference was founded in 1951 to negotiate compensation for Jewish victims of the Nazi regime. It uses some of the proceeds to assist victims of Nazi persecution.

Two claims were filed by a Hans Hitzegrad and a Werner Szosta. Strangely enough, they both listed their address as my family's house in Berlin-Karlshorst.

Another was from a Ruth Levy. In a letter to the Berlin authorities, she made a claim for the house that "the Nazi government had taken away from my parents, Theodor and Helene Simonsohn in 1942 [sic]."[16]

That wasn't possible. My father had *bought* the house.

Then my lawyer sent me a copy of the 1941 entry for the house in the *Grundbuch*, the German register of real estate. The notary who handled the sales contract asked Theodor Israel[17] Simonsohn and my father to identify themselves, which they did with identity cards. Then, on a page headed by an eagle clutching a swastika, the notary added: "Those present made a declaration about themselves, that *Herr* Simonsohn is a *Jude* and that *Herr* Heise is an *Arian*."

I was in shock.

---

[16] Actually in was in early 1941 that the house was sold. However, at this point Mrs. Levy was 90 years old.

[17] The Nazis forced Jewish men to add the name Israel as their middle name; women were required to add the name Sarah as their middle name, and their passports where stamped with a large J.

My father a Nazi who extorted property from a Jewish owner? I couldn't believe it. Reading that sentence was the second most chilling moment in my quest to reclaim ownership of the house. *The most* chilling moment came several years later and brought me closer to the Holocaust horrors then I had ever been.

With the revelation that the house had been bought from a Jew, my lawyer's interest in the case waned overnight. A close friend in Berlin, Helfried Geissler, recommended another lawyer in the city. We went to see him and I explained the case to him. He assured me he would get right on it, and I executed a power of attorney so he could handle the case on my behalf. I never heard from him; my phone calls and faxes went unanswered.

By now more than six years had passed and I had made little progress, other than to get a copy of the real estate register and the names of the other claimants.

I fired both lawyers in 1997.

I was close to giving up. But, dammit, it was my house, and I simply did not believe that my father would in any way participate in the Nazis' persecution of Jews. It was not a matter of money, but of principle — and nothing is more ferocious than a fight for a principle.

When I was running out of patience, my friend Geissler in 1997 came up with the name of another attorney: Gunnar Schnabel. He became, as I affectionately called him (but never to his face) my "junkyard dog." He took on the challenges of the case with a deep knowledge of the applicable laws, imagination, determination, unswerving perseverance and ferocity when the moment called for it.

Schnabel, like his Spartan black, white and chrome office on Berlin's Kurfürstendamm, was all business: "Let's look at the facts."

And fact No. 1 was that under German law all property sold by a Jewish owner between 1933 and 1945 was presumed to have been sold under duress, rendering the sale invalid. And the burden of proof that my father had not forced a Jew to sell his house in 1941 was mine.

Such proof, Schnabel said, was virtually impossible to establish because of the tough standards of the law. From the real estate documents, we knew what the house had sold for, and experts agreed that it was a fair market price at the time. The contract also showed that my father paid an additional 500 *Reichsmarks* for pieces of inventory in the house that were listed in a separate document that was not attached to the contract.

The law also required proof that the money my father paid for the house had actually gone to the seller, Mr. Simonsohn, not the Nazi coffers. How to prove that? The contract from the real estate register specified in detail how the payment was to be made to the notary, who would hold it until the sale was closed and registered in the *Grundbuch*.[18] But Ruth Levy had maintained that her family never received any money.

Everyone was dead, and I had no relevant records. The only record I had at the moment was the faded color picture of the house with the front dormer window half open. There was another record that I would not find until much later.

The third requirement was proof that my father "in special ways and with considerable success" saw to it that the Simonsohns received their money, for example, by getting the money out of Germany, a requirement that was virtually impossible to meet because, under the Nazis, it was a crime to take money out of the country without authorization from the government.

There were two paths we could pursue, Schnabel said. One was to take the fight to the

---

[18] That is still standard procedure in Germany, where notaries play a much broader role in real estate transactions than in the United States. Indeed, most real estate transactions are usually handled by a notary, not a lawyer, which is the custom in the United States.

German courts. But he predicted that that would be a long — perhaps 10-year long — process because there were hundreds of thousands of cases like mine. And he reiterated that "it would be expensive and the outcome, given that the house was bought from a Jew, highly uncertain." Meanwhile, the condition of the house — which we later found needed tens of thousands of dollars in repairs — would worsen since the house would be under governmental administration. "If we win in 10 years," Schnabel said, "the house might be close to a ruin."

The only viable solution, according to Schnabel, was to work out an agreement acceptable to the Simonsohns' heirs and the German courts. With that, the quest to get the house back took a whole new turn: Find the heirs.

## 9: Reunion With My Little Girlfriend

**By J. Arthur Heise**

While dealing with the two hapless lawyers and finding Schnabel, I visited the house twice. The first time was in 1992. My friend Geissler; his fiancée; my wife, Simine; and I drove to Berlin-Karlshorst on a beautiful spring day.

Before driving to the house, I told them of my memories of the house, including the bomb that took a chunk out of the apartment house behind our house and the cellar window through which I had peeked at the Soviet tanks and troops that terrorized my family.

When we came close to the area where the house should have been, we got lost. Then I saw a huge oak growing out of an island in the middle of *Neuwieder Strasse*, the street where the house sits. I instantly knew where we were. "Make a right; it's that house over there."

**That's the oak tree that instantly led Art to point to *das Haus.***

The house looked much as I remembered it, except that the stucco needed a coat of paint, weathered windows needed to be replaced, and the roof did not look very tight. But everything that I had talked about — the chunk missing from the apartment house was still missing and the small coal cellar window through which I peeked at the Soviet troops — was precisely as I remembered it.

I was taking pictures of the house from every angle, when Simine came up to me and whispered, "There's a woman across the street that keeps looking at you." I didn't want to turn around. Simine came back a few minutes later and said, "Now there is a man with her." I still didn't turn around, because it had not been unusual for neighbors to become unfriendly when strangers came around taking pictures of homes that might belong to them and planned to kick out the current tenant.

Finally the woman put down her gardening tools, came through her front gate and asked, *"Bist Du Jürgen Heise?"* (Are you Jürgen Heise?)[19]

How could she possibly know me?

---

[19] The J in my name stands for Jürgen, which many Americans either have a hard time pronouncing or made fun of when I was young. Thus, when I was in high school in the United States, I switched to my middle name and became Arthur and, in American fashion, Art for short.

It turned out that she had met my mother in the late 1970s. *Mutti* stopped by to look at the house, and so Elli H. had learned that my brother and father had died and knew that I was the only surviving child. From that, she deduced that I had to be Jürgen Heise. Elli was one of the group of small children I had played with as a little boy. But Elli and I were special friends, who often were at each other's house. Although I did not immediately recognize her, I was stunned to meet her again after more than a half-century had passed.

When I said yes, she immediately invited us to her house for coffee. Since it was a warm spring day, we sat around a table in her backyard, where her husband joined us as we began our journey of remembrance. Later, when she took us inside the house to show us the sunroom where we had played, she caught Simine glancing questioningly at the front door, which had various wooden patches on it. Elli caught the look and explained that those patches covered the places where Russian rifle butts had splintered the door in 1945. A new door, she said, was impossible to buy during the decades of the DDR.

Elli H. is not her real name. During an interview for this book, she asked that I not use her real name because she was concerned about repercussions should the book reach Germany. Evidently, 40 years of *Stasi*-controlled life has not been entirely erased. The *Stasi (Staatssicherheitsdienst)* was the dreaded East German secret police. Indeed, she told me during that interview that after we had coffee in her backyard in 1992, a neighbor, a former *Stasi*, immediately showed up to find out who we were. She said she should have told him that the days of everyone in East Germany being spied on were over, but she simply said we were friends whom she hadn't seen for a time.

Elli told us that after her family was forced out of their house, they ended up in what turned out to be East Germany. She described years of privation and a life with little opportunity. At first, her family — like mine —lived with her grandmother. When her father returned from an American prisoner-of-war camp, he found them at his mother's house. He also went through the struggle of finding a place to stay in bombed-out Berlin, but eventually found a small apartment in what became East Berlin. After Elli graduated from secondary school, she, in the German tradition, took an apprenticeship, and worked as a saleswoman in various government-operated organizations. Her husband worked as an engineer, but that's all she would say about him. "You know it's still so... I don't know, I shouldn't say anything."

In 1958, the Soviets moved the barbed-wire fence back one block as they moved out of the houses on that part of *Neuwieder Strasse.* Elli and her family, because they had lived in East Berlin, were allowed to move back into their home.

When I heard all that, I realized how lucky I had been that the apartment my father found was one block inside the American Sector. Instead of leading a dreary life in the East, I had a generally happy life in America. What a difference one city block can make.

When I mentioned to Elli that one of the families living in the house, the Szostas, had been in touch with me about buying the house, she lowered her voice and said: "Be careful. He was a big *Bonze* (big wig) in the *Stasi*," the dreaded East German secret police. "Be very careful dealing with him," she repeated. Szosta later told me that he had worked for the East German postal system.

She said the Hitzegrads, the family that rented the upstairs apartment in the house, also had held high positions in the East German government's Sports Association, the organization infamous for introducing performance-enhancing drugs on a large scale. (I have no reason to believe the Hitzegrads participated in the use of performance-enhancing drugs.) Because of those positions, they too had been given what by East German standards was good housing.

When I explained to Elli that I was working to get the house back, she was delighted. She explained that before the Wall came down, people like the Szostas and Hitzegrads would strut through a store and she would lower her head and make herself small. "And when you run into them in a store today, they act as if what they did was perfectly normal." She urged me not to give up trying to regain the house. "I want to see the *Bonzen* thrown out one day," she said. I promised her that I would keep at it, even if it took years.

She also took us for a walk through the neighborhood. At the end of the *Neuwieder Strasse,* she pointed to a white house that had child-like scenes painted on it. The windows were tightly shuddered. From the outside, it looked like a daycare center. Not so. She said it had been where the *Stasi* held and tortured some of those it had arrested.

**As of 2004, the chunk of the apartment house torn out by a bomb behind the homemade air raid shelter in which Art, his family and neighbors survived was still missing.**

We also walked along the street with the three-story apartment house. The chunk that was taken out by the bomb while we were in the homemade air raid shelter was still missing. Elli pointed to the corrugated metal sheets that had been used to board up the adjacent parts of the building. "They had nearly 50 years to rebuild it," Elli said

157

sarcastically, "but the 'efficient' DDR never got around to it." (As of 2013, the missing section had still not been replaced by the owner; instead the double lot has been converted into a small park.)

Not only was the visit with my former childhood playmate pleasant, but it also turned out to be fruitful. The first lawyer I had hired lacked the competence to find the most critical document we needed, the *Grundbuch* (real estate register) in which the house sale was recorded. Elli said she knew exactly where to find it. At my request, she contacted the lawyer so he could secure the needed *Grundbuch* excerpt.

Four years later, we went back to Berlin to show the house to my 32-year-old son, Mark, who had not been to Germany as a grownup. The second reason was that Szosta had contacted me again to indicate his continuing interest in buying the house.

At Szosta's invitation, we got to see the interior. The Szosta apartment was surprisingly well-furnished, mostly Danish in style. Apparently being a *Bonze* in the *Stasi* had its advantages. But the house also had problems. There were water stains from leaks in the roof. The kitchens and bathrooms needed updating and, Szosta told me, the 60-year-old windows, and the electrical and heating systems all had problems.

Going down to the basement was eerie. There was the coal cellar that had sheltered all those women and small children and the window from which I had watched the Soviet soldiers. The frame of the backdoor still had the nail holes from the time my father nailed the door shut a half-century ago. The *Sickergrube* (the former septic tank my father had converted to a wine cellar) had been found — despite the cow dung that had covered it — and emptied of its valuable contents. By whom, Elli had no idea, but she suspected the Russians because they had been in the house for the first dozen or so years. The air raid shelter in the backyard where I thought we would all be crushed to death had been filled in.

Szosta pressed me on the sale of the house. There was little I could tell him other than that its return to me was taking much longer than I had hoped. It would be another year before I found the "junkyard dog" and at his direction started the search for the Simonsohn heirs.

## 10: Finding the Heirs

### By J. Arthur Heise

Ruth Levy's address was easy enough to find — it was in her letter to the city of Berlin and the resulting claims form. Of all the places she could have lived in the world, her address was in Tamarac, Florida -- only about 30 miles from my home then in Miami.

But how to approach her? Do I, Art Heise, walk up to her home and introduce myself as the son of the *Herr* Heise she was sure was the Nazi who had forced her parents out of their house and not paid for it? My wife and I drove the 30 miles to Tamarac on a Sunday in 1997 and cruised around the neighborhood like potential house buyers. But we did not have the nerve to stop to see if anyone was home.

Having started a public opinion research operation at my university that interviewed people over the telephone, I knew that strangers were more likely to talk to a woman than a man over the phone. So Simine volunteered to call. Ruth Levy was not available; she had died three years ago; so had her daughter Susanne, four months after her mother's death. Did Ruth Levy have any other heirs?

You need to talk to Melanie Murphy, the unidentified woman on the phone said. (I found out later that she was the new wife of the late Susanne Levy's former husband, Alvin Kuhr.) When my wife told her that she was calling about a house in Germany, the woman quickly invited us to lunch so that we could discuss the matter. But my wife insisted on getting an address and phone number for Melanie Murphy, who was Ruth Levy's granddaughter and Theodor and Helene Simonsohns' great-granddaughter. She lived in Plano, Texas, outside Dallas. (Melanie Murphy was her name at the time. After a divorce in 2009, she resumed using her maiden name, Melanie Kuhr.)

So in the fall of 1997 I began a series of phone calls with Melanie. She knew little about the house, only that her grandmother had received a $1,600 check from the West German government as restitution for the loss of their rights to education and disruption to their lives.

I explained to her that, on the basis of the contract contained in the *Grundbuch*, my father had bought the house from the Simonsohns in 1941 at a fair price and that I was pursuing its return to my family's sole living heir, me. I described the poor condition of the house, and I told her about the cost of the lawyer I had hired (and the two I fired); about the various trips I had made to Germany so far to get the house back; and that it could take up to $25,000 in lawyers' fees before the house was returned plus considerable repair expenses.

Melanie was reserved but polite on the telephone. The lawyer Schnabel had suggested that I offer her $25,000 in exchange for her signing over to me any rights she might have to the house. Melanie was very cool to that proposal. I did not hear from her for weeks. Eventually she rejected the $25,000 offer.

In late 1997, I had a business trip scheduled to the University of Texas, Austin, which would take me through the Dallas-Fort Worth International Airport (DFW). I suggested that we meet there face-to-face. With some reluctance, Melanie agreed.

As I stepped off American Airlines flight 1768 at DFW on the morning of November 21, 1997, a slender, attractive blonde — in her mid-30s, I guessed — greeted me with a sign that read "Art Heise."

On the phone, we had agreed that each of us would bring whatever relevant documents we had. We found a quiet corner in the American Airlines Admirals Club where her 7-month-old son Andrew could continue to nap in his stroller as we talked.

Halting small talk at first. Awkward pauses. Slowly we got around to the house. She, too, had pictures of the house, with Theodor and

Helene in front of it when the first story was up; with Theodor, Helene and Melanie's grandmother, Ruth, admiring it from the side when only the roof was missing; and, finally, a picture of a smiling Theodor resting his hand on the front gate of his finished house. And there was another picture, shot from precisely the same angle, with the same dormer window half-open, just as in the faded one that had hung in my parents' bedroom in Syracuse — the picture that my mother had grabbed when we were forced out of the house in 1945.

I walked her through the files and *Grundbuch* excerpt that I had for the house, pointing out the financial details in the contract, including the total payment of 37,500 *Reichsmarks* for the house and some of its contents.

Melanie showed me a typewritten note from her grandmother about one of her attempts to have the house returned to her. Written in the late 1980s, it was in English and apparently aimed at a newspaper. In the note, Ruth Levy said that her parents were forced to sell the house by the Nazis, that the money went to a lawyer and that her parents never saw a penny. She wrote further that her parents briefly moved to an apartment after the sale of the house and were shortly afterward arrested by the Gestapo — on their 49th wedding anniversary.

That's when Melanie pulled two red-rimmed documents from a file. They were the death certificates of Theodor and Helene Simonsohn. They perished in Theresienstadt concentration camp, he on December 15, 1942 — allegedly of "paralysis cordis" (heart attack) — she on February 22, 1943 — allegedly of "Angina pectoris" (coronary artery disease).

It was *the* most chilling moment in the quest to get the house back when I realized that the couple from whom my father had bought the house perished in a concentration camp within two years of the sale.

Although Melanie had told me on the phone that her great-grandparents died in

Theresienstadt (Terezin in Czech), it stung to my marrow to see the actual death certificates.

Theresienstadt had been a cynical farce perpetrated by the Nazis on Jews, who were told it was a "model ghetto" for mostly elderly Jews. The Nazis went so far as to dupe some elderly Jews into thinking they were going to a spa or resort. "Many elderly actually paid large sums of money for a nice location in their new home."[20] The town of Terezin had a population of approximately 7,000 in 1940 and was clustered around two fortresses built in 1780. In 1941, the Nazis sent two transports of Jewish workers to convert the former garrison town into a concentration camp that "needed to hold about 35,000 to 60,000." Soon the Theresienstadt residents were evacuated to make room. The first Jews deported to Theresienstadt were Czech, but Austrian, German, Danish and Dutch Jews soon joined them. Upon arrival, they were stripped of all

---

[20] This section draws extensively on *Theresienstadt: The 'Model' Ghetto*. Jewish Virtual Library at *http://www.us-israel.org/jsource/Holocaust/terezintro.html*.

their belongings. Even before the camp population reached its height,

> [t]he allotted space per person was two square yards — this included per person usage/need for lavatory, kitchen and storage space. The living/sleeping areas were covered with vermin. These pests included, but certainly were not limited to, rats, fleas, flies and lice…. The food scarcity affected the elderly the most. Lack of nourishment, lack of medicines and general susceptibility to illness made their fatality extremely high.

Because of the high death rate, a crematorium was added in 1942. While there was no gas chamber, 190 bodies were cremated a day. When the end of the war neared and Nazis were trying to erase the traces of what they had wrought, 8,000 cardboard boxes filled with ashes were dumped into a pit and another 17,000 into a nearby river.

But most of the Theresienstadt prisoners did not perish in Theresienstadt but in killing camps such as Auschwitz-Birkenau. Transports carrying from 1,000 to 5,000 Jews were regularly sent east to the killing camps.

Theresienstadt is perhaps best known for the great charade the Nazis perpetrated on the Danish and Swedish Red Cross. These organizations began asking questions after the first Danish Jews had been sent to Theresienstadt. The Nazis decided to take this opportunity to convince the world that "Jews were living under humane conditions." They spruced up the town with fresh turf, benches and flowers. They went so far as to create Hollywood-like facades. Among other things, they had a bakery operating or hung a sign that read "Boys School" — which no boy ever attended. After seeing these phony attractions, the Red Cross delegation concluded that the Jews were being treated humanely. "After the visit, the Nazis were so impressed with their propaganda feat that they decided to make a film."[21]

When my wife and I visited Theresienstadt in 2004, it was still a grim town. In the main square, a few blades of grass fought for survival in the dust. Paint was peeling and plaster was crumbling on the apartment buildings along the square. Many of the approximately 200,000 Jewish men, women and children who passed through *Theresienstadt* had been squeezed into those buildings. The two fortresses looked as if the inhabitants had left a few weeks ago and all that had been done was to sweep them clean. The few locals we passed on the street stared straight ahead and made it clear with their body language that they did not want to be bothered. It just seemed incomprehensible that, for example, of 15,000 Jewish children who had passed through the camp, only 132 survived Theresienstadt.

---

[21] See *Theresienstadt: The 'Model' Ghetto,* Jewish Virtual Library.

There was a small museum. What captured our attention were the handmade costumes — mostly burlap — that the inmates had produced for plays and operas they put on. Indeed, at one point there were so many musicians in the Theresienstadt concentration camp that "there could have been two full symphony orchestras performing simultaneously daily."

But what I was looking for was any kind of trace of the Simonsohns. Their names were not among the hundreds carved into the wood of a room that's part of the Terezin Memorial. And we could not find registers of those who had passed through Theresienstadt. One problem was that none of the attendants spoke German, French or English, only Czech. It seemed that the few staff members who were on hand were there simply to collect a paycheck.

The Simonsohns perished here and simply vanished — at least for a time. It was some time later that the Czech National Archives prepared a website that listed the Simonsohns among the people who had perished in Theresienstadt.[22]

The only uplifting part of our visit to Theresienstadt was to see a dozen buses full of high school students from nearby Germany. We chatted with several and learned that they were there as part of their social studies classes that dealt with the-never-to-be-forgotten Holocaust.

I knew little of all that about Theresienstadt as I chatted with Melanie in the American Airlines lounge. I was so stunned that day in 1997 by the Theresienstadt death certificates that it took me a while to get around to one of the main issues I wanted to raise at the meeting.

After Melanie rejected the $25,000 offer for her rights in the Karlshorst house, Schnabel suggested a new strategy. I would ask her to sign jointly with me a declaration that assigned

---

[22] See www.terezinstudies.cz/eng/ITI/databases/databases.

all of her rights in the property to me. That declaration was aimed at the German courts. To protect her rights, she and I would sign a separate agreement spelling out how we would share proceeds from the sale of the house. I reminded her again of the perils that awaited us if we started a battle between ourselves for the ownership of the house; that it could take up to 10 years for the case to wend its way through the German courts; that it would cost tens of thousands of dollars in lawyer fees; and that one of us may end up with a ruin.

We parted on friendly terms. Little Andrew was still snoozing.

*Das Haus*

## 11: **Melanie's Reaction**

### By Melanie Kuhr

I had driven to DFW Airport that November morning in 1997 both curious and apprehensive. Who was this Art Heise? He had sounded all right over the telephone, but what would he really be like? I had thought about taking my husband along, but, as usual, he was away on a business trip. So I took my baby, Andrew, now 7 months, in his stroller. If I felt I had to make a quick departure, I could always use him as an excuse.

After I met with Art in the Admirals Club at the airport, I slowly walked to the parking lot, feeling a bit surreal. A range of random emotions and thoughts flowed through me.

I don't know what I expected, but Art was a real person, well-dressed, well-spoken and polite. He was my brothers' age. In contrast, not long before meeting Art I had met with two former East Germans who had sought me out because they claimed I owned part of an apartment house in the former East Berlin, an apartment house that had been owned by my mother's paternal grandmother, Minna Levy. And they had struck me as real con artists when I met with them in the lobby of the Dallas Hilton. Seems like these Germans were coming out of the woodwork with real estate "deals." Instinctively, I did not trust any one of them.

This photo was taken around the time when Art and Melanie met at DFW Airport, and she brought along Andrew as her escape insurance. Her daughter Allison is on the right.

Art seemed none of that. I felt pervasively sad after Art told me of his experience as a small boy when his family was kicked out of the house on *Neuwieder Strasse* and the nightmares of the Battle for Berlin that he had lived through.

But I never felt any anger toward him. I never thought, "Oh my gosh, he's a Nazi." I thought he too was unlucky, just like my Mom. Their childhoods were disrupted by the moral and physical disintegration of their society. Thoughts flashed through my mind: What if his father was in the Gestapo and was the person my grandmother had told me about — the one who kept pounding on their door and threatened that unless my great-grandfather paid him so much a month, he would burn down the house? And I remembered my grandmother telling me that one day my great-grandparents had to leave the house with their worldly possessions and memories in only one suitcase, leaving everything else behind.

Art showed me a photo of the house identical to the one my Om had left me. How was that possible? Had there been copies of the photo? Did his mother find a copy when they assumed possession of the home and its contents from my great-grandparents? This is when the feeling started ... how could Art and I ever really know? What really transpired now lay in ashes.

177

I've always gone through life giving people the benefit of the doubt. I've been burned big time by that attitude a few times, but on the whole I think it is a healthy way to live.

However, I put the brakes on after meeting Art. There were so many unknowns. I was so outside my comfort zone of knowing what the real information was. I couldn't really get myself to believe Art, because I didn't know him. And not only that, it was a fact that contracts on houses sold by Jewish owners to non-Jews in 1942 were null and void. The sales were presumed under current German law to have been made under duress, and I felt this was true for Theodor and Helene when they sold the house. I had no idea whose team he was on, but likely not mine. I felt I was in a territory totally unbeknownst to me. The stakes were high because I wanted to do the right thing for Susanne and Ruth and my great-grandparents. At the same time, I kept thinking about how you can make something good out of something so bad. There are no winners here. Although one or both of us may end up with the house and the proceeds from it, nothing could compensate for the pain the inhabitants of *das Haus* experienced. I came home, calmed down and determined that I had to find out the truth.

*Das Haus*

## 12: The Interminable Back-and-Forth

### By J. Arthur Heise

It would be two months, mid-January 1998, before I would hear from Melanie after our meeting at DFW Airport. She had consulted with various people and asked me to share with her copies of the documents I had unearthed in Germany. She was sure she could get copies on her own, but that it would save valuable time if I supplied them. After "an individual in Washington, D.C., that is knowledgeable in these matters" has reviewed the documents, "I will either assist you or proceed with reclaiming the property," she wrote.

(She had indeed contacted the proper authority in Germany about the house. But the German agency, as I later learned, in its acknowledgement of her claim told her that all further correspondence must be in German.)

She concluded the letter by writing, "My only desire is that there be an honorable settlement of this property to its rightful owner, should that be you, I will provide what is necessary to expedite your acquisition of the house in Karlshorst...."

Within a week, I sent her a copy of every document I had. From that date on, I also sent her copies of every bit of correspondence related to the return of the house. Transparency became my mission. Since many of the letters and faxes were in German, I also either summarized them for her or, if they were of particular importance, translated them in whole. But in my response, I also wrote:

> Everything that I know about the sale of the house in Berlin-Karlshorst indicates that my father paid a reasonable price for the property and otherwise conducted himself decently in the sale of the house. If you or anyone else has proof that I am wrong, I will immediately sign any document, appear in any court, do whatever needs to be done to make

sure the property is returned to your family forthwith.

Given the horrendous insanity which caused us to meet more than half a century after the paths of our forebears crossed, let's you and I work together to do what is right.

My letter met with weeks of silence. Little did I realize that this was the beginning of a tug-of-war — at least that's how I perceived it at the time — that would last for months. In March, Schnabel in Berlin became impatient, wanting to know what was going on.

It was not until June 1998 — seven months after our meeting at the Dallas airport — that Melanie finally agreed to work with me on the return of the house. But it was just the beginning of more back-and-forth between us.

For one thing, the German consulate in Dallas told Melanie that the house was much more valuable than the 300,000 to 400,000 *Deutsche Marks* (then $174,000 to $232,000) I had mentioned to Melanie. I based those numbers on an informal estimate from a German real estate agent who placed the value of the house in that range.

That was not enough for Melanie. She firmly insisted on an appraisal of the house. She was under the impression that real estate appraisals in Germany work pretty much as they do in the United States. Not so. A *"Gutachten"* (expert opinion) is executed by a licensed appraiser, in this case a certified engineer. That is the German practice. And it is not cheap. The cost was about $1,360 that, at first, Melanie wanted me to pay. Later she agreed that we would divide the cost of the appraisal and would split all the other costs. After discounting for necessary repairs, the appraisal came in at exactly 400,000 *Deutsche Mark* (DM) or about $232,000 at the exchange rate at the time.

Then there was the financial split if the house could be sold. Because of all the time and money I had spent on four trips to Germany, I proposed a 70/30 split in my favor, with me absorbing all my travel and legal costs (which ran to $21,000 for five trips, not counting legal fees). She wanted 50/50, including a split along those lines of the legal and travel costs. We eventually agreed on a 55/45 split in my favor to recognize the time I had put into the process over the years.

And after agreeing with the contract my U.S. lawyer and hers had drawn up regarding the splitting of the proceeds, she had new problems with it. And so it went.

Meanwhile, another problem had arisen in Berlin, one the Jewish Claims Commission was likely to pounce on. Since the Simonsohns had bought the property on which they built the house, the question was, the lawyer Schnabel pointed out, from whom had they bought the land in 1935 on which the house was built?

That, of course, raises the question of why a Jew would buy property in 1935 to build house in Nazi Germany. After all, from the moment Hitler came to power in 1933, anti-Semitism had been expressed in various laws and actions, codified in the vicious 1935 Nuremberg laws. Of the approximately 525,000 Jews who lived in Germany in 1933, about one-third had left before the horrific *Kristallnacht in* Germany and Austria in November 1938. Another third left in the months after the *Kristallnacht*. "Of the estimated 164,000 who were still within the Third Reich in the autumn of 1941, 123,000 — or less than a quarter of the original community in the early 1930s — perished in the camps.[23]

Why did some Jews stay? I have found the best answer to that haunting question in Victor Klemperer's diaries of the Nazi years.[24] Their families had lived in Germany for generations, many had served with distinction in the German army in World War I, and most of them considered themselves Germans first and Jews second. As Klemperer wrote on May 30, 1942: "Perhaps it is not at all up to us to go,

---

[23] John V. H. Dippel, *Bound to the Wheel of Fire: Why So Many Jews Made the Tragic Decision to Remain in Nazi Germany* (New York: Basic Books, 1996) 255-56.

[24] Victor Klemperer, *I Will Bear Witness: A Diary of the Nazi Years, 1933-41,* (New York: Random House, 1998), and a second volume by the same name and publisher covering the years 1942-45.

but rather to wait: I am German and am waiting for the Germans to come back; they have gone to ground somewhere."

"This mad man Hitler couldn't possibly last,"[25] was not an uncommon attitude among German Jews.

So there was the troubling question hanging over the purchase of the land and the construction of the house. If the Simonsohns, even though they were Jewish, had bought the property in 1935 from a Jew, under the current German duress law, that person — neither Melanie nor I — was entitled to the property.

Back to Germany I went. With the help of my friend Helfried Geissler, it took us days to find out that the East German government — under which private property was not allowed — had stored all the old East Berlin-area real estate records in a castle somewhere in East Germany. But the Berlin government was in the process of bringing the records back to the

[25] Mark Jonathan Harris, *Into the Arms of Stranger: Stories of the Kindertransport,* a documentary, 2000.

city, to be archived in a former IBM factory. Luckily, the Berlin-Karlshorst records were already there. Apparently the Simonsohn property had been part of a large tract of land owned by a farm family and subdivided for housing starting in the Twenties. I was able to track the record back to 1865, without a sign that any member of that family had been Jewish, largely on the basis of their last name, Sange.

Before I left for Germany and upon my return, I called Melanie several times but there was always another reason for delay. In the meantime, I received another call from Szosta indicating he was still interested in buying the house. His continuing interest was essential in being able to sell the house, because under German law it was virtually impossible to evict a tenant. And who would want to buy a house that had two tenants whose low rent was controlled by the government and which would largely be used to make repairs to the house? But if one of the tenants bought the house, then he could, if he so chose, evict the other tenant. Again I had to put Szosta off because I was not yet the owner of the property.

By December 1998 — more than a year since we met at Dallas-Fort Worth International Airport — I reached the edge. It seemed clear to me that Melanie did not fully trust me. I can't say I blame her. After all, I was the son of the "Nazi" who her grandmother claimed stole the house from her family. At the same time, I had been completely open with her since we met at the airport. I was further frustrated by the endless hours I was spending corresponding with Schnabel, Melanie, the German consulate, Szosta and others.

That's why I finally wrote Melanie that I was ready to sign my rights in the house over to her if she was prepared to take the lead. And I agreed to a 50/50 split because of the hours and expense she would face. But I also warned her of the obstacles she faced. She would have to find an attorney in Germany; hire a translator to accompany her as she dealt with the various bureaucrats and so on. I also wrote:

> Obviously I have reached the end of the rope. I leave it to you how you would like to proceed. As I have said again and again, there is no way that this matter can be worked out without a certain amount of trust between you and me....

> Having said that, you need to know that I will no longer work on redrafting agreements and consulting with expensive attorneys without some certainty where all of this is going. My time is too valuable and limited. ***The ball is entirely in your court.***

> **Please don't misunderstand me. My *strong* preference is still to work together with you in the recovery and sale of the property in Berlin-Karlshorst. But it has to be done in a business-like manner — with the modicum of trust**

such undertakings require — that puts a stop to the back-and-forth of the last several weeks. (Emphasis in original.)

*Das Haus*

## 13. Melanie's Search for the Facts

**By Melanie Kuhr**

How could I have known at the time I was growing up that my family's story was so special, different, historic, bitter sweet?

We only know what we know. And now after the meeting with Art at the airport, I was sorry. I was so sorry that I had not recorded the stories, paid more attention, cared about what had been. I was too caught up in me and did not know it. Now I do.

**Melanie and friend.**

I've seen it in my kids — a cursory interest in the past, but all so caught up in the process of growing up, learning, having fun, friends, camp, grade school, high school, college, jobs, getting married, having children, building careers and all the life lived in between.

Now I understand the horror, fear, shock, disbelief, anger, and the plethora of other feelings that my family and millions of others experienced. How I wished that my mother and grandmother were alive so I could ask, listen, record, investigate, and pursue their stories. Interview them like I interviewed applicants for jobs, dive deep into the nitty-gritty.

And had I paid close attention to their stories, in all likelihood I still wouldn't know everything.. It was a life that was a generation past and one my ancestors quietly tucked away just like the backpack and the teddy bear mother kept in the steamer trunk.

As Art had promised, he promptly sent me copies of all relevant documents and correspondence, especially with the lawyer Schnabel, most of which were in German. He either translated the material in full or summarized it for me. It kept piling up on my desk. Sure, there were official documents, transcripts, piles of faxes I received regularly from Art. And they meant nothing to me; the documents that piled up were likely no more than a substantiation of one person's truth.

Also adding to my doubt and distrust was the $25,000 the lawyer Schnabel had suggested Art pay me for my rights in the house. I had no idea whether that was a fair sum or not, but it struck me as very low. In any case, the matter was not one of money; I wanted to know the truth about the "sale" of the house from the Simonsohns to the Heises. I did not want to repeat the past, and I wanted to do the right thing by my mother, grandmother and great-grandparents. So I rejected the $25,000 offer, and for the first time really started to feel. I felt anger, shame, betrayal, remorse, regret; and I didn't know why.

I did not know if I really wanted to engage in this; I wished Art had never found me; I wished the whole story would fade away like the documents and the pictures. Just gone. Yet, despite my misgivings, I chose to participate in the "deal"; I had to know the truth, and if possible, to see that the Simonsohns, my *Om* and my mother received some justice for all that they endured.

Eventually, I brought my professional, analytical side to bear and prioritized what needed to be discovered and done. I put together a plan, and first on the list was to find people who might remember.

Ruth, Susanne and, later, I kept in correspondence with Ursula Wellemin. Ursula was a second cousin to Ruth Levy. Ursula's father, Manfred, was the son of Gustav Hess, the brother of Helene Simonsohn and the owner of the paint factory Theodor represented.

Ruth and Susanne did not even know that Ursula, her sister Louise and their parents, Manfred and Gertrud, made it to London in 1939. Manfred had been sent to Buchenwald, but was released, and they lived in England during and after the war. Ruth received a letter from the Jewish Refugees Committee in December 1954, informing her that her cousin Manfred Hess was searching for her in England.

I sent a letter to Ursula in December 1997. I knew from Ruth that Ursula and John were in the process of reclaiming properties in the Dresden/Pirna area of Saxony and Gotha (Thuringia), belonging to Ursula's mother. They had hired local lawyers who had been working on their claims since the early 1990s.

John sent me an extensive letter in January 1998, in response to mine. The letter began: "Melanie is not to accept a derisory offer from the son of the German 'buyer' of her great-grandparents' Berlin house. German law recognizes that sales of Jewish property after a certain date was carried out under duress and therefore is not legal and that therefore, restitution to the original owners or their legal heirs should take place ... and restitution should be vigorously pursued, particularly for property in Berlin. Contact the German Consulate in Houston they may put forth some lawyers and information regarding restitution matters. You must proceed very cautiously."

In April 1998, I met Ursula and her husband, John Wellemin, in London for tea at the

Marriott County Hall. I was in London on a trip with Eric, who had spent the past year traveling to London on a consulting engagement. John himself had an amazing story, as did so many people in Europe. John moved to London in June 1939 from Prague. He joined the Czech brigade in England during the war and returned to Prague. He then had to escape from the Communists in Prague in 1948 and returned to London.

I met John and Ursula in the lobby. I had never even seen a picture of them and yet when Ursula, then 73 years old, walked into the lobby, I knew immediately who she was — a Hess. The resemblance to my grandmother Ruth was startling. The same stature, petite frame, silvery white hair, striking eyes, and a presence — the same proud, confident, polite, and cultured way Ruth carried herself.

The three of us spent a couple of hours over tea, and it was as though I had a brief moment to sit at the table again with *Om* and ask some of the questions I wished I had asked so long ago. Ursula shared mostly stories of her immediate family; after all, she was a young girl when she last saw Ruth. Yet she remembered receiving a beautiful hand-knitted yellow sweater from her. She said that, before the Nazis, life was lovely in Dresden, Berlin and Ermsleben. Ursula did confirm that my great-grandfather, Theodor Simonsohn, had indeed been a representative for the Hess paint company, a firm owned by my great-grandmother's brother, Gustav Hess.

We discussed the letter John sent in January and he was adamant that I should proceed with caution. The house belonged to my family legally and morally, and if I chose to work with "the Nazi" that was my choice. I could not help but wonder if I was doing something wrong, and I felt sure the legal wrangling would benefit only the lawyers. And, more important, I believed something good had to come out of this meeting with destiny.

Later, my lawyer in Dallas and his senior partner, who had worked on some cases similar to mine, also suggested I proceed with extreme caution. They, too, were aware that there were various parties floating around the United

States looking for people — especially Jews — who were the legitimate owners of property in the former East Germany so they could try to buy the rights on the cheap. I was told the same thing by the German consulate staff in Dallas. So far, no one thought I was doing the right thing. Yet I still felt Art was as much a victim as my mother..

When we lived in Tamarac, my *Om* had kept all sorts of belongings in the steamer trunk my mother had taken out of Germany in 1939. When my father, Alvin Kuhr, remarried, I took everything I could out of the trunk, put it in boxes and took it to Texas, where I lived at the time. I grabbed whatever papers I could and some little figurines, knitted sweaters and so forth. But I didn't go through everything because there was so much stuff, including dozens of old opera programs.

My father remarried on Christmas Eve 1995 — 17 months after my mother died. The woman he married, Sylvia, discarded or more likely sold grandmother's steamer trunk, so I never had a chance to go through whatever remained.

Sylvia is the woman who answered the phone when Art's wife, Simine, called the house in Tamarac looking for Ruth Levy. Sylvia could smell money and stopped at nothing to get her hands on it.

When my mother was in her last days, she said to me, "Don't worry about your Dad; he'll find himself a real cookie." He did, and he deserved it. On my mother's deathbed, all he was concerned with was "what is to become of me." Typical of him to think only of himself. My father ended up in the Willow Wood nursing home in Fort Lauderdale, all of his money siphoned off by Sylvia to her family. Unable to speak, his tongue atrophied, cared for by two paid caregivers, he was without any of his children or grandchildren. He was alone, penniless and likely heartbroken, not knowing why his family had moved on without him as a part of our lives. Karma.

Once home, I started going through the various papers. The only relevant items I found were the letter my grandmother had sent to the Berlin government staking her claim to the house and another letter that she apparently wrote to a newspaper. In both, she claimed that the Nazis took the house away from the Simonsohns and that they were never paid. How she knew that, since she had left for England in 1939 and the house was sold in 1941, remains a mystery. There was no existing correspondence to clarify it. But in the beginning, when Ruth and Susanne had gone to England, letters could still cross borders and likely Theodor and Helene wrote of these details to Ruth.

On the other hand, Art had unearthed the sales contract that Theodor Simonsohn had executed. The contract provided that, in addition to the sales price, the Simonsohns would get the apartment in which Art's parents had lived. That, I was told, was a highly unusual, friendly gesture for the times. According to the contract, Art's father paid my great-grandparents 500 Reichsmarks for some items in the house. But my grandmother had clearly told me that her parents left the house with only their personal items and that everything else remained in the house. I suppose the Russians eventually pilfered the contents.

I contacted the Jewish Claims Conference, which was the authority in Berlin and New York that dealt with cases like mine. I also wrote to the Restitution Authority in Berlin; they promptly responded that all further correspondence would have to be in German, a language I could not speak.

There was one thing, however, that I absolutely insisted on and that was an appraisal of the house as it stood. Art had told me that a real estate friend of his in Germany had informally placed the price at 300,000 to 400,000 DM, depending on its condition. I wanted objective and certifiable information, and even then I was doubtful we would get an accurate accounting. When the appraisal came in, it placed the value at exactly 400,000 DM; that fact added to Art's credibility in my eyes. At some point, you have to trust people.

Another factor that weighed heavily on me was the letter Art had sent me in which he said that if anyone had proof that his father had extorted the house, "I will immediately sign any document, appear in any court, do whatever needs to be done to make sure the property is returned to your family forthwith."

Time passed, lots of time, in a tedious back-and-forth between Art and me during this fact-finding period. I began to see Art more as a

man searching for answers. I saw he had an insatiable desire to learn the truth and resolve the doubts he'd carried with him so long. And he was a family man; he spoke of Simine and his son, Mark, adoringly. In short, I had come to see Art as someone who was trying to do the right thing under

**Art and his wife, Simine.**

very difficult circumstances.

Art saw my sometimes weeks-long silences as a tug-of-war. My delays in responding were not calculated; they were due to the personal demands on my time.

I had a full-time job with EDS, managing 240 employees from East Coast to West. I had a husband whose work took him all over the world. And I had two children, an au pair and a household to manage.

But I understood Art's frustration. He had worked on getting the house back for six years, and any further progress rested in my hands. I also understood that time was of the essence since we had a potential buyer who could withdraw at any moment.

At the end of December 1998, I called Art. Based on Art's actions and the documents he had unearthed, I decided to focus on the good in people and decided to work with Art as a partner. Working collaboratively was the solution that saved us time and resources. I hoped he understood my frustration in coming to grips with this complicated situation.

*Das Haus*

## 14: Victory at Last — Maybe

**By J. Arthur Heise**

Plenty of issues remained, but Melanie and I were now cooperating fully and in a timely manner on all of them.

The first and most important issue — and now the easiest — was the written agreement between Melanie and me. It had been drawn up by my son, Mark, who is a lawyer, and was reviewed by Melanie's attorney in Dallas. After a few minor changes, we signed it and had it witnessed in mid-January 1999. It spelled out in three pages of detail that she would sign over to me her rights in the Karlshorst house and that we would split the proceeds 55/45 in my favor after all legal and other costs had been paid.

The second major issue we had to address was to prove that Melanie was the legitimate heir to the Simonsohns and I to my parents.

In my case, the matter was straightforward. My parents' wills had been probated in

Syracuse, New York, and obtaining copies was routine — until the officially translated wills were presented to a Berlin court. But what seemed a simple, straightforward matter, came with a hurdle; in retrospect, a humorous hurdle. The Berlin court was not satisfied because the wills did not contain an official ink stamp. It took Schnabel to explain to the court that embossed seals were routine for U.S. courts. To show the court that the document was indeed official, he literally had to hold the wills up against light and run his finger over the seal. With that bagatelle out of the way, the German court issued the all-important *Erbschein* — Certificate of Inheritance — that made it official that I was indeed my parents' heir.

Proving that Melanie was the legitimate heir of the Simonsohns was another matter. Through the courts in Broward County, Florida, she had little difficulty obtaining Ruth Levy's will, which made Melanie the sole heir of her grandmother's estate. The problem was finding proof that Ruth Levy was in fact the heir of the Simonsohns, who had perished in the Theresienstadt concentration camp. Schnabel, our lawyer in Berlin, explained that given the circumstances of the Simonsohns' deaths, there were legal ways to obtain an *Erbschein* showing that Ruth Levy was the true heir. But he also pointed out that it would be a tedious and time-consuming process, something that could cause our potential buyer, Werner Szosta, to sour on buying the house.

Melanie thoroughly searched all of her grandmother's papers but found no *Erbschein*.

Schnabel being Schnabel, he remembered my telling him that Ruth Levy had in 1976 applied to the West German government for restitution for the Karlshorst house and had received about $1,600. That she had received payment indicated to him that she had been able to prove to the German authorities that she was the Simonsohns' legitimate heir. And that meant there was an *Erbschein* for her filed away somewhere in Berlin. It took Schnabel, the junkyard dog, three months, but he found the critical Certificate of Inheritance for Ruth Levy in the bowels of the German bureaucracy.

The German courts required something more for Melanie to sign over her rights in the house to me — an *Abtretungserklärung,* a Declaration of Assignment. Since we now had all of the Certificates of Inheritance, translated wills, birth and death certificates — paying significant fees along the way — we were finally in the position to obtain the Declaration of Assignment.

We mistakenly thought that the honorary German consul in Dallas could execute the document. Not so. Well, what about the German consulate in Houston? It did not have a Foreign Service officer of sufficiently high rank to certify the Declaration. So in June 1999, Melanie had to fly to Miami so that the Declaration could be executed in front of a German Foreign Service officer of the appropriate rank.

The best part of Melanie's visit was that we had the opportunity to have an enjoyable lunch at Miami's Intercontinental Hotel, which was only a few blocks from the German consulate. She met Simine for the first time at that lunch, and the two women had a pleasant conversation. After Melanie's return home, she sent a short note that ended by saying, "Perhaps next time we'll share some champagne."

Clearly the relationship had taken a 180-degree turn, from suspicion and mistrust to cooperation and trust.

*Das Haus*

## 15: Bombshells

by J. Arthur Heise

With a duly certified Declaration of Assignment, Gunnar Schnabel could now approach the Berlin authorities to request that the *Grundbuch* be changed to show that the ownership of the house had passed from my father to me. We were now in a position to sell the house to Werner Szosta, who was still interested in buying it. While Szosta had offered 420,000 DM, Melanie and I agreed that the price should be 430,000 DM because of the improved real estate market in Berlin

As it turned out, anything but smooth sailing lay ahead.

Not long after Melanie had visited Miami, the first bombshell dropped in mid-July 1999 when the Jewish Claims Conference informed the German authorities that it was objecting to — and thereby blocking — the sale of the Karlshorst property. My research going back to 1865 into the origins of the property on which the house was built proved to be of critical importance.

It was sold in 1935 by a family named Sange, but there was no indication that the Sanges were Jewish. Also for various legal reasons, Schnabel also did not believe that the JCC had a case. He laid that out in a letter to the JCC, concluding, "[I]t cannot be that the heiress of persecuted Jews, who in [1942 and 1943] perished in the Nazi [concentration camps], receives no restitution today because the JCC in a general request without any evidence seeks to stop the sale of the property and thereby prevents restitution."

Within a week, the JCC informed Schnabel that it was withdrawing its objection.

That was only one of the events that made for rough sailing when Melanie and I thought we had entered calmer waters.

For one thing, the purported buyer, Werner Szosta, no longer lived in the Karlshorst house, and hadn't done so since 1992, when he had moved to a house outside Berlin — a fact he had kept from me. Instead, as the lawyer Schnabel discovered, he had sublet part of his and his wife's apartment to a Hans-Günter Löwe, a musician, allegedly in the band of the Felix Dzershinsky Guards Regiment that was also part of the *Stasi.* And it turned out that Löwe was the one who actually wanted to buy the house. Szosta was his front man.[26] As my childhood friend Elli put it, "They all worked for the same 'Firma' (company)" — the *Stasi.*

As long as Löwe had the money, that was fine with Melanie and me. Schnabel went ahead and, as is German custom, had a notary prepare a sales contract for the house with the price set at 430,000 DM. It was completed but not signed in October 1999. The holdup was that Löwe allegedly needed time to arrange the financing of the purchase.

A second bombshell fell a month later, this time tossed by Löwe. He wrote Schnabel that he was

---

[26] I asked both Löwe and Szosta for interviews for this book. Neither replied to my request.

withdrawing his offer of 430,000 DM. He gave two reasons: First, that the required repairs would be more costly than specified in the sworn appraisal Melanie and I had commissioned; second, that it would be much more difficult to evict the renters of the other apartment than Schnabel had led him to believe. However, he concluded that if I "were still interested in negotiations, [he] would be prepared to buy the property and house at a price of 350,000 DM."

At that, the junkyard dog bared his teeth and went on a legal tear. As far as Schnabel was concerned, the entire delay — namely Löwe's alleged difficulties in obtaining financing — was part of a stratagem to buy the house for a lower price. Elli's warning about dealing with former *Stasi Bonzen* rang in my ears.

But Schnabel had discovered documents that showed that neither the Szostas nor the other renters had legal rental agreements. The rental contracts for the two apartments were held by the central administration of the former East

German Dynamo Sports Club under authority of the *Stasi*. (An administrative unit of the government of the unified Germany had assumed control of all of these agreements after the Wall went down.) According to Schnabel, the documents also showed that Szosta had worked at *Stasi* headquarters.

Schnabel further told Szosta that the subletting of the apartment was no longer valid because the subletting agreement had expired in January 1999.

Then he dropped his own bombshell. Given that Löwe and Szosta had no legal rental agreement and because of the illegal subletting of the apartment to Löwe, he told them to vacate the apartment within one week. If they didn't, he would take them to court to enforce the eviction.

But he also dropped a very clear hint that another reason for his action was that he knew the five-month delay by Löwe was nothing but a ruse to buy the house for 80,000 DM less than he and Szosta had agreed five months earlier.

In a similar letter, he also gave Löwe one week to vacate the apartment he was illegally subletting from Szosta. If he didn't comply, Schnabel would take him to court.

Schnabel's tactic worked. Within a couple of weeks, both Szosta and Löwe were pleading with him not to take them to court. I was furious at Löwe's and Szosta's scheming, and so was Melanie. But I was more so because it had looked like after all the years I had spent on the seemingly never-ending battle to regain the house, it was finally over. Löwe — and his *Stasi* assistant Szosta, as Schnabel called him — had to pay.

On behalf of Melanie and me, I told Schnabel that the sum of $430,000 DM we had agreed to earlier was no longer acceptable, given the delay and the extra work it had created for Schnabel. The five-month delay also had cost Melanie and me serious money because of the declining value of the dollar. Had the original contract for 430,000 DM been executed in a timely manner, we would not have lost 7.2 percent because of the decline of the dollar. If they don't comply, I told Schnabel, tell Löwe and Szosta that we will see them in court. We *may* entertain an offer of 450,000 DM, I wrote Schnabel, provided Löwe agreed to that in writing within five days.

Two days past the deadline I had set, Löwe signed the sales contract — after some negotiating with Schnabel and with Melanie's and my consent — for 440,000 DM.

The money was paid to the notary, but under German law he could not disburse it until the transaction was formally entered in the *Grundbuch.* That would take several months, Schnabel advised, which was delayed further by the fact that Löwe was not able to make a final payment of 10,000 DM until June 2000.

Meanwhile, Löwe's chicanery did not cease. Contrary to the terms of the sales contract, he decided to take it upon himself to waive the rent from the two apartments, which were owed to me until the house sale closed. Schnabel did not like that at all. He gave Löwe one week to pay the rent money. Löwe ignored him. That was a big mistake. Schnabel sued him and won. In the end, it cost Löwe $2,658, which Melanie and I split 55/45.

In June 2000 — almost exactly 10 years after I had started the battle to get the house back — Melanie and I received the payments we had agreed on. The long quest for *das Haus* was finally over. Melanie and I are have not yet shared that bottle of champagne, but she sent Simine and me two candleholders from Neiman Marcus. They grace the cocktail table in our sunroom, reminding me daily of a warm friendship.

## 16: Nazi Bonze or Not?

**By J. Arthur Heise**

For me, one critical question was still open: Was my father a swaggering Nazi in a long black leather coat who had forced the Simonsohns out of the Karlshorst house and not paid them?

The contract for the sale of the house between my father and Theodor Simonsohn suggests in three ways that this was not the case.

For one thing, the contract specified in detail how the money paid was to be distributed to Simonsohn.

Second, according to experts consulted by the lawyer Schnabel, the price paid reflected the fair market value at the time.

Third, the contract specified that my parents would trade their nearby apartment with the Simonsohns. Schnabel had always considered that a friendly gesture between two cooperating parties. Because of the perennial shortage of housing in Berlin, the gesture was especially important, because it would assure that the Simonsohns — for whom, as Jews, finding housing would be especially difficult — would have a decent place to live.

But that was all circumstantial evidence. I was looking for more solid proof. Ruth Levy, after all, had insisted that the Simonsohns never received any money for the house.

On a visit to friends in Berlin in 2004, I called Schnabel to find out if he knew where and if any documentation about my father's denazification proceedings might exist. He didn't know but referred me to an archivist friend of his. That's simple, she told me, just go to a Berlin government building on the *Wittenberg Platz,* right in the heart of the city, and they should have the file in their archives.

Ironically, the building was just a few blocks from our hotel. We had walked past it at least a dozen times.

When Simine and I arrived at the archives, a friendly young man asked what I was looking for. I told him, and he asked for my father's full name, his birth date and his last address in Berlin. And he wanted to see my passport.

He disappeared for about 15 minutes and returned with a file in his hand. He asked me to look at the file to verify that it contained what I was looking for — my father's denazification proceedings. It did. I asked for a copy and the young man took off again and five minutes later handed me the copy, free of charge.

As soon as we left the building I started scanning the file. I was so nervous that I didn't even realize that a slight drizzle was falling. Simine grabbed me by the sleeve and dragged me into the nearby *KaDeWe*, a huge department store with a nice restaurant on the top floor.

I studied the file carefully. The proceeding, under the auspices of the American military government, had taken place before the

Denazification Commission Kreuzberg (the section of Berlin where my father's business was situated and where we lived after the war) on September 11, 1947.

The commission had interrogated three witnesses under oath before the proceeding. Three others were questioned under oath at the hearing, as was my father.

The three witnesses who had been interrogated before the proceedings all testified that during the Hitler period, my father neither worked for nor supported the Nazi Party. The testimony of one witness, Hermann Mueller, carried extra weight because he was an *Opfer des Faschismus* (*ODF*), a victim of fascism. (Why he was designated an *ODF* is not made clear in the document. Generally, someone was designated an *ODF* because he or she had actively resisted the Nazis and suffered for it.)

During his sworn testimony, my father pointed out that the electrical equipment company, then still owned by his elderly and ill father, did 70 to 80 percent of its business with the public gas company. "Out of fear that the gas company might withdraw its orders, the applicant joined the party, but he never held office or rank in the party and was never active on behalf of the party." The proceedings also note:

> Because the applicant did not actively participate in party matters he was expelled from the party in 1944, prior to the assassination attempt [on Hitler]. The business employed circa five persons, including no foreigners or Jews. In 1941 the applicant purchased a property from a Jew; through documents he could prove that the Jews took possession of the monies paid.

If I had had those documents that proved my father paid the money due the Simonsohns, I would have slept better many a night.

The first of the witnesses who appeared before the commission, a Karl Fischer, testified that he had known my father professionally because they were in the same business. Fischer had spent some time in Russia, so he was under constant police observation "for lack of political reliability." He told the commission that often he could not complete all the work assigned to him by the Nazis and he passed a great deal of that work on to my father so that the Nazis would not accuse Fischer of sabotage by delaying the work. Fischer also testified that

> During this period he would have political discussion with the applicant [my father] from time to time and never had the suspicion that the applicant was a party member, something he learned from the applicant only shortly before the end of the Nazi era. At that time the applicant showed him a document from the party that established that Heise was expelled from the party in the year '44

because of favoritism toward Jews and non-participation in party activities.

The second witness to testify before the commission, Herta Vater, said that for a time she had lived in the same house as my parents and had "never witnessed that the applicant wore a uniform or that he wore the party emblem; she also never observed that the applicant proselytized for the party. During relevant conversations H[eise] spoke against the positions of the Nazi Party, so that one never had the suspicion that he was a Nazi."

The third witness, Siegfried Tembrock,

> was a neighbor of the applicant in Karlshorst and testified that the purchase of the property from the Jew was carried out to the satisfaction of the same. The Jew even [after the sale] continued to have friendly relations with H[eise]. It was known to the witness that the applicant joined the party and [he] therefore exercised a certain caution in

the beginning; as time went by he noticed, however, that the applicant did not have Nazi tendencies because he did not proselytize for the party and did not actively participate in its affairs. Because he did not own a radio himself, the applicant frequently informed him of news carried by foreign radio stations.

(Listening to foreign radio stations was an offense that could easily result in a trip to a concentration camp.)

So there it was, as good an answer as I was likely to get to the question that had troubled me for more than a dozen years. My father had not been a fervent Nazi; indeed, he was eventually kicked out of the party; apparently he had a good relationship with the Simonsohns after he bought their house; and he had provided documents to prove that they had received the monies due them.

\*\*\*

We finished our coffee and pastries in the KaDeWe and stepped outside. The drizzle had stopped, and the sun was shining.

But was the sun shining on a *Persilschein*, as sardonic Berliners called these papers? They called them *"Persil"* certificates after the name of a popular German laundry detergent that removed "brown stains."[27]

I did not think so. For one thing, the hearing had been held in the American sector, and the Americans were much more thorough than the other Allies regarding denazification. Their hearing commission had gone to the trouble to send an investigator to interrogate three of the witnesses in person, under oath. My father had to testify under oath and produce documents that he had actually paid for the Simohnsons' house. Three other witnesses were interrogated under oath at the hearing. He never held a position in the party, never advocated for it and, because of that, was

---

[27] Perry Biddiscome, *The Denazification of Germany: A History 1945-50* (Stroud, U.K.: Tempus Publishing, Ltd., 2007) 72.

thrown out of the Nazi Party in 1944, they testified.

My father testified that he joined the party because he did 70 to 80 percent of his business with the municipal gas company and was afraid to lose that business. In addition, the remainder of his business was building and repairing electrical motors and electrical switching gear for various customers, primarily private businesses. Because of the work he did for the gas company and some other government units, his small factory was declared essential to the war effort. And of his five employees, none were forced laborers nor Jews.

Another benefit, however, of his business being declared essential to the war effort, was that he did not have to serve in the military. In 1939, my father was 37 years old, prime age for service in the German armed forces. So instead of being sent to kill on Nazi Germany's various battlefronts or in concentration camps, he was home to help his family get through the war.

But no matter how I analyze — rationalize? — the situation, he was a Nazi who through his work supported the Nazi machine.

I have been asked why he and the family did not simply leave Germany. That's a question asked with imperfect hindsight. Between 1933 and the beginning of World War II, it was Hitler's policy to drive the Jews out of Germany. [28] But emigration for non-Jewish Germans was very difficult. All emigrants — Jewish or not — could take only 10 *Reichsmarks* out of the country. If they wanted to take more than that, they had to get government approval and pay a special tax, which started at 20 percent but eventually reached 96 percent. [29] More important, the Nazis were not keen on letting able-bodied men leave the country. Even if a person

---

[28] Martin Dean, *Robbing the Jews: The Confiscation of Jewish Property in the Holocaust, 1933-1945* (Cambridge, U.K.: Cambridge University Press, 2008) 79.
[29] *Ibid*, p. 61.

obtained a visa to leave, there was the question of where to go. Many countries, including the United States, had extremely limited immigration quotas in those days.

I have wrestled with this issue ever since I obtained my father's denazification documents and, on a more abstract level, for years before. I have discussed it *ad nauseam* with people knowledgeable about this period of history. I have read much of the extensive literature about the Hitler years. I learned about the Versailles Treaty, which was despised by the Germans and used by Hitler to whip them into a frenzy, of the Great Depression that struck Germany with a fury, the problems of the Weimar Republic, the anti-Semitism in Germany, Austria, Poland, the former Soviet Union, elsewhere in Europe and, yes, albeit to a lesser degree, in the United States. In short, I learned *what* Hitler did and *how* the Holocaust came about.

Perhaps all of these factors combined provide an answer to *why* it was possible for Hitler to unleash the most horrible event in modern history — the Holocaust. But I am not certain of that. I think the historians have more work to do to answer the question of *why*. What I am certain of is that I — as a 6-year old at the end of WWII — was not responsible for what Hitler wrought. But I am even more certain that I — nay, all of us — are responsible for making sure it never happens again.

Obviously, I would much prefer that my father had never joined the Nazi Party. But I did not walk in his shoes during a time when the slightest misstep could result in an interrogation by the *Gestapo* and a trip to a concentration camp

Few of us have perfect fathers. I loved mine, imperfect as he was, for many reasons. He risked his life to protect his family, he provided for us in the brutal years after the war, and he brought us to America at the earliest opportunity. Most of all, I loved him because he — though not a demonstrative person — clearly loved me.

*Das Haus*

## 17: Was the Odyssey Worth It?

### By J. Arthur Heise and Melanie Kuhr

*While the money we -- Melanie and Art -- received in the sale of das Haus was not insubstantial, it was not what drove either of us in the quest to have the house returned to us.*

*Far from it.*

For me, Melanie, the deepest concern was to do the right thing by my great-grandparents, grandmother and mother, who were all victims of the Holocaust, directly or indirectly. The question that wouldn't go away was: If all real estate contracts between Jews and non-Jews were considered null and void, why was the sale of *das Haus* any different? But I ended where I began, believing that Art was as much a victim of the atrocities of the time as my family. It took a lot of soul-searching for me to decide to cooperate with Art, something Art misinterpreted as delaying tactics. But I finally decided that in cooperating in the return of the house, I could honor my family by selling the house once and for all, and this time not under any circumstances other than free will. I donated some of the money to Hadassah, the women's Zionist organization, which promotes empowerment, advocacy and a connection to Jews worldwide.

On a spiritual level, the 10-year battle for the house further strengthened my commitment to living a Jewish life. Neither my mother nor grandmother had been observant; in Germany they were not afforded the right to live a Jewish life; and later, after the war, they could not understand how a God could allow something as repulsive as the Holocaust. Yet from Ruth and Susanne, I experienced and embraced the Hebrew principle *tikkun olam,* which suggests that it's our shared responsibility to heal the world.

Once I went to college, I became distant from the Jewish life that I had lived at home. Indeed, I married outside the faith and had three children with my husband, whom I later divorced for reasons that had nothing to do with Judaism. But during the quest for *das Haus*, I became more comfortable living my Jewish life as much outwardly as I did inwardly, and I embraced the culture and shared it with my children. This would serve as an affirmation that the Jewish people would continue to thrive in spite of the persecution and hatred that still exists in the world today.

\* \* \*

For me, Art, the quest for the house and the research for this book brought something approaching closure to several issues that had troubled me greatly.

The first among these issues was what kind of Nazi my father had been. With everyone involved dead, my discovery of my father's denazification hearing record — which found him to be a mere "nominal" member of the Nazi Party — was a partial answer, but I nevertheless remain troubled that my father was a member of the Nazi Party. There are many reasons that may justify his decision. But as I have noted, few fathers are perfect. And I loved *Vati* for all the good he did for his family during and after the war, including bringing us to America at the earliest opportunity.

The most troubling for me was Melanie's grandmother's assertion that the house was taken by a Nazi and that her great-grandparents never saw a penny. But there were no documents among the many left by Ruth Levy, Melanie's grandmother, that attest to that claim. Furthermore, communication between Germany and England was extremely limited during the wartime years when Ruth was in England. So how would she know what happened in Berlin-Karlshorst in 1941? One possibility is that Ruth remained in contact through the 1950s with Minna Levy, her mother-in-law, and her brother-in-law Emil Levy, after he returned to Berlin from the labor camps. Somehow they weathered the Nazi scourge.

Ruth Levy is probably partially correct, but it is also highly likely that my *Vati* paid for the house what it was worth at the time.

That contradictory conclusion is based on an email interview I conducted with a senior researcher at the U.S. Holocaust Memorial Museum, Martin Dean. What Ruth Levy probably did not know is that all Jewish bank accounts were "blocked" by the Nazis, allowing the owner of the account to withdraw only small monthly stipends on which they lived and additional amounts only in cases of medical or other emergencies. As Dean wrote to me,

> I would imagine that according to the contract [for the sale of the house] the money was probably paid or at least owed to the former Jewish owner, but would, of course, have been paid into a blocked account, such that the supposed beneficiaries had no real access to more than a fraction of these funds. The matter is further complicated by the deportation to Theresienstadt, as many

Jews sent to Theresienstadt from Germany were obliged to sign over most of the remaining wealth to the Gestapo in a so-called *"Heimeinkaufvertrag"* (Home Purchase Contract), which was supposedly going to pay their living costs while in the Old People's Ghetto of Theresienstadt.... *Suffice it to say that the money was probably paid, but the main beneficiary was almost certainly the German state.* (Emphasis added.)[30]

In other words, it is entirely possible that my father paid for the house but that the Simonsohns saw little if any of the money.

What still troubles me was my initial relationship with Melanie. I knew enough about the German "bounty hunters" who were flooding the United States after the Wall came down, looking especially for Jews who owned property in the former East Germany.

---

30 Email interview with Martin Dean, Applied Research Scholar, U.S. Holocaust Memorial Museum, Washington, D.C., November 25-26, 2012. For further details see Martin Dean, *Robbing the Jews: Confiscation of Jewish Property in the Holocaust, 1933-1945* (Cambridge, U.K.: Cambridge University Press, 2008).

I refused to be measured by that standard. As far as I was concerned, there was a legitimate dispute over the ownership of *das Haus*. I had emotional attachments to the house because I grew up in it and had some terrifying memories of what it was like to live there. And there were documents that showed that my father paid a fair price for it.

Because I met Melanie only once face-to-face, under very stressful circumstances, Melanie and I never had a chance to have a long talk in which we could take each other's measure, not just in words, but facial expressions, body language and all the rest. All communication aside from the DFW encounter was via fax, email or telephone.

But Melanie was extremely busy with her job and raising her family. I, Art, also had a demanding job building a school of journalism and constantly traveling to Central America to strengthen journalism in that part of the world.

As a result, what I completely missed was the strain that Melanie was facing when it came to *das Haus*. I figured out only recently, during the writing of this book, that for Melanie it was not just a matter of a piece of real estate, but was about her family's struggle in Nazi Germany and the rediscovery of her Jewish roots. She wanted to make sure that her mothers', her grandmother's and her great-grandparents' memories were honored properly. That misunderstanding in large part caused me to erroneously think she was engaging in delaying tactics, when, in fact, she was in emotional turmoil.

Those discoveries alone made the odyssey for the house worthwhile.

*** 

*In preparing this book, dozens of times we bemoaned our failure to raise the subject more often in our earlier years — Art with his parents, Melanie with her mother and grandmother. In Melanie's case, neither*

*Susanne nor Ruth spoke often of the events leading to the loss of the house. Also, when Melanie was old enough to have asked questions, she was away and busy with college and, later, her hectic professional career and family. My, Art's, situation was similar. Like many Germans their age, my parents did not often speak of the Hitler era, including the loss of the house in Karlshorst. What made it worse was my almost anti-German attitude in the Fifties and Sixties. When my parents said something about Germany, I either ignored it or, if it was positive, belittled it.*

*Had we, Melanie and Art, had those conversations, how much more would we have learned, good or bad? Would it have made us more antagonistic toward each other or would we have learned to trust each other sooner?*

*\*\*\**

*But both of us agree that the odyssey was worth it for a reason that outranks all others: We worked hard to overcome the reservations we had about each other. Over a long period of time, we learned to trust each other, mainly by being honest with one another. With that approach, we learned that antagonists can, in time, become good friends.*

**We hope you liked the book. Please write a review on Amazon.com.**

# Acknowledgements

Art wants to thank these folks for their help with the book: My grandchildren, Jane, Jackson and Finnegan, who were the primary motivation for writing my part of the book;

Art's motivators: From the top, Jane, Jackson and Finnegan

Michael Hart, for coming up with the concept for the cover; Jorge Arteaga, for executing the design of the cover of the book; Charles H. Green for his perceptive critique of the first draft; Mark Heise, for his helpful suggestions;

Simine Heise, for her suggestions and, more important, her patience with the project; Lana Hendershott, for her careful review of the manuscript; Michael Huber, for his painstaking editing; Joe Kuhr, for his perceptive critiques; Rick Panadero, for his suggestions; David Swanson, for some critical input; and Marion Liddell for, as always, seeing what I overlooked; Harold and Anita Watsky for their unwavering support. Above all, I thank Melanie Kuhr for agreeing to join me in this adventure.

*\*\*\**

Melanie dedicates this book to the late Ruth Levy and Susanne Levy Kuhr for their courage and unconditional love, and to her children Allison, Andrew and Alexander; strong kids from a strong line.

**Melanie's children: From left to right, Alexander, Andrew and Allison.**

Melanie wants to express her sincere thanks to Art Heise for his research, his dedication, his patience and his encouragement; when I wavered, he was my rock. And I'd like to thank my nephew, Joe Kuhr, for his time, his editing, his candor and his coaching.

*Das Haus*

27803341R00146

Made in the USA
Lexington, KY
27 November 2013